G. WARREN NUTTER

The

Strange World

of

Ivan Ivanov

AMERICAN INSTITUTE FOR ECONOMIC RESEARCH

The Strange World of Ivan Ivanov

By G. Warren Nutter

With an Introduction by Phillip W. Magness

ISBN: 978-1-63-069191-2

Cover art: Vanessa Mendozzi

G. WARREN NUTTER

The Strange World of Ivan Ivanov

AIER | AMERICAN INSTITUTE *for* ECONOMIC RESEARCH

To Coleman, Terry, Anne, and William

Preface

This little book had its origin in a series of articles commissioned by the Philadelphia *Inquirer* and designed to describe, in simple language, how life differs for the common man in the Soviet Union and the United States. It is not intended to be an authoritative treatise or a probing analysis of the two societies in all their relevant aspects, but rather a bold sketch of the contrasts between the two systems and how they affect the lives of ordinary citizens. Conditions in the Soviet Union naturally receive more scrutiny, since those here, bad as well as good, are better known to the reader.

I am particularly grateful to David Appel, feature editor of the Philadelphia *Inquirer*, and Charles Maddock, chairman of the American Bar Association's Standing Committee on Education About Communism and Its Contrast with Liberty Under Law, for encouraging me to undertake this task and supporting me in it. Mr. Jeremiah McKenna and Professors Kazimierz Gryzbowski, Peter Low, Branko Peselj, and Charles K. Woltz were very helpful in providing information on the nature of the legal systems in the two countries. Needless to say, they should not be held accountable for what I have written on the subject.

I am indebted to Marie-Christine MacAndrew for helping with research and editorial work, to John Echols for assisting her, and to Maxine Maupin for typing the manuscript.

G. Warren Nutter
Charlottesville, Virginia
May 1, 1968

Contents

Introduction

For much of the twentieth century, leading figures of the American academy looked upon the Soviet Union's economic performance with what may be legitimately described as a sense of credulous envy. Although the Soviet economy was smaller than the United States', the Soviets' official numbers consistently projected a growth rate that would soon overtake their Cold War rival's and, in doing so, validate the claimed inevitability of the socialist economic system on which it was built. Even as American economists rejected the Marxist philosophy behind Soviet planning, they settled into a curious postwar habit of disseminating economic projections that depicted the Soviet economy overtaking the United States in the near future.

Beginning with the 1961 edition of his bestselling economics textbook, Paul Samuelson included a graphic displaying the comparative growth rates of the American and Soviet economies. Per this forecast, the Soviet gross national product would overtake the United States at some point between twenty-three and thirty-six years in the future. Curiously, by the 1980 edition of the textbook this same graph had shifted forward by two decades so that the point of projected intersection would still take place between twenty-two and thirty-two years in the future. Similar claims appeared in competing textbooks from the time and generally transferred over into the specialist literature on the Soviet economy as well.[1]

At the midcentury mark, economist G. Warren Nutter (1923–79) provided one of the lone dissenting voices to challenge what had become a matter of conventional wisdom among Sovietologists. Whereas others perceived vibrancy and vitality in the socialist society's industrial growth, Nutter recognized its long-term economic decline concealed behind a politically crafted veneer of propaganda about socialist industrial prowess. From 1956 onward, he labored on providing a statistical corrective that painted a picture of a society gradually succumbing to the weight of its own central planning and the wasteful accretions of a graft-riddled and politically repressive bureaucracy.[2] The early reception of Nutter's work expressed doubt about its accuracy compared to more optimistic portrayals from the textbooks and accompanying Sovietology literature, yet history proved him right. Nutter had scooped the field and accurately identified

---

1 Levy, David M., and Sandra J. Peart. "Soviet growth and American textbooks: An endogenous past." *Journal of Economic Behavior & Organization* 78.1-2 (2011): 110-125.

2 Nutter, G. Warren. "Some observations on Soviet industrial growth." *The American Economic Review* 47.2 (1957): 618-630; Nutter, G. Warren, Israel Borenstein, and Adam Kaufman. "Growth of industrial production in the Soviet Union." *NBER Books* (1962).

an economy with deep structural problems—most of them directly traceable to its destruction of a functional price mechanism through the tools of state management.

Nutter's assessment was no abstraction, but rather the result of years of close study of the relationship between state policy and industrial concentration in the United States—the subject of his dissertation at the University of Chicago. But he also possessed an uncommonly keen eye for extracting observations from his surroundings. He deployed the latter during a twenty-eight-day visit to the Soviet Union in 1956 as a self-described "tourist" researcher, which he contrasted with other American experts whose longer visits occurred under the heavy scrutiny and management of handlers from the Soviet government.[3] Whereas others largely picked up on what the Soviets wanted them to see and incorporated curated factory tours and contrived statistical claims into their assessments, Nutter apparently had a knack for looking beneath the surface through everyday observations of his surroundings—simply by keeping an eye on the types of goods in the shop window, the patterns of workers entering the factory in the background, and the way that the people he encountered described even the most mundane economic

---

3 Levy, David M., and Sandra J. Peart. "G. Warren Nutter's 'Traveler's tale of the Soviet economy': A witness to the actual world." *The Review of Austrian Economics* 28.4 (2015): 397-404.

transactions of their daily lives.[4]

He had no formal training in Russian and does not appear to have claimed fluency, describing his tour as having taken place "under the severe handicap of not knowing the language."[5] Yet Nutter was also something of a linguistic autodidact—an ability he realized in the US Army during the liberation of Europe a little over a decade prior. In reading his travelogue, one gathers that he may have gleaned more from observing the surrounding conversations than he let on—more than, importantly, his Soviet guides realized at the time.

Born in Topeka, Kansas, to a Jewish mother who was widowed around the time of his birth, Nutter grew up in tight economic circumstances. His small family migrated around the Depression-era rural Midwest in search of stable income, eventually settling in Iowa. A promising student, he received a break to attend the University of Chicago, where he came under the mentorship of the economist Henry Simons as an undergraduate.

Nutter's wartime service took him to the front lines of the European theater. He fought in the infantry during the invasion of Germany, directly witnessing the horrifying revelations that came with the liberation of the Nazi concentration camps. He returned to

---

4 Ibid.

5 Nutter, G. Warren. 1956. "A Traveler's Tale of the Soviet Economy." September. Manuscript located at the Dwight D. Eisenhower Presidential library.

Acknowledgement and thanks to David M. Levy, who provided me with a copy.

Chicago after the war with the intention of completing his graduate studies under Simons, but the latter's untimely death and an existing acquaintance with law professor Aaron Director brought him under the guidance of a newly hired economics professor by the name of Milton Friedman. Graduating in 1949, he became Friedman's first doctoral student to enter into academic life. After a brief stint on the economics faculty at Yale, he eventually settled at the University of Virginia, where he cofounded the Thomas Jefferson Center for the Study of Political Economy with his old Chicago classmate James M. Buchanan.

The dissolution of the Soviet Union, membership in a star-studded faculty that included two future Nobel Prize winners (Buchanan and Ronald Coase), and an untimely death from cancer in 1979 have somewhat overshadowed Nutter's own substantial resume as a scholar. Curiously, as we mark thirty years since the fall of the Berlin Wall, political calls for socialism have regained fashionability on the far left. Rehabilitated by academics and activists who present themselves as "democratic" expositors of centralized planning, practitioners of the modern euphemized version are all too eager to dissociate their brand from its notorious and deadly twentieth-century iterations. Thus the recent anniversary of Karl Marx's two-hundredth birthday was met with an outpouring of editorials and academic commentaries celebrating the claimed relevance of the discredited philosopher's theories for "solving" income inequality, climate change, and a slew of similar progressive political causes in the present day. The human toll imposed by his followers received comparatively little attention, as did the connection between this recurring pattern and the socialist philosophy that undergirds it.

Yet this year marks another anniversary that may, in part, provide a needed intellectual corrective to the misguided fancies of the ongoing socialist rehabilitation. Whereas Nutter's earlier work on the Soviet Union consisted of detailed industrial analysis and number crunching suited for academic discussions among economists, in 1969 he turned his attention to the more practical matter of daily life under a socialist system of government. The result was *The Strange World of Ivan Ivanov*, a short yet hard-hitting indictment of the economic and political repression that so often follows from attempts to structure a society around Marxist ideology and centralized economic planning.

Nutter began his work on *Ivan Ivanov* in 1967 as part of a debate with the Marxist historian Herbert Aptheker at the University of Western Ontario. As was a common theme at the time, Aptheker enlisted the history of racial segregation in the United States to build a sweeping indictment of "capitalism" as an economic system, including assigning it blame for inculcating racial and other forms of discrimination. Nutter's rejoinder "I Choose Capitalism" is published here as an accompanying text to the book for the first time.

The counterargument did not shy from confronting the problem of racism in the United States. Yet as Nutter explained, discrimination appeared to be a persistent curse of the human condition. Far from solving this problem, the socialist approach of the Soviets had actually systematized it into the instruments of the state.

Noting that state action carries with it a far greater degree of coercive power, Nutter reframed the question of discrimination by asking his audience to judge a society on whether it availed the individual of a means to escape the very same instruments. In the Soviet Union, state policy had become a means of carrying out anti-Semitic and other ethnic persecutions under the guise of economic redistribution, property appropriation, and even genocidal persecutions and famines. Though Nutter avoided implicating his opponent by name, Aptheker himself had weathered the Stalin years as something of an apologist for the Soviet state's most notorious atrocities.

The cheerful depictions of life under socialism that the Marxist intellectual presented amounted to a political sleight of hand. They entailed a false comparison between an idealized form of egalitarian socioeconomic organization, as proposed on the far left but never realized, and the observed faults of Western capitalism as it existed. Aptheker was comparing a constructed socialist fantasy to a disliked capitalist reality and declaring that fantasy the victor on account of its unrealized promises. Yet as Nutter stressed, the reality of life under socialism often reduced society to abject impoverishment and immiseration.

Far from being "solved" by socialism's promises, discrimination on ethnic and religious lines, along with deeply inegalitarian political distributions of resources and power, were endemic features of the Soviet system. Even as these features also manifested in the West through private and state-sanctioned discrimination, capitalism itself was an escape mechanism to the very same problems that the Soviet state, through its absolute and uncontested control of social life, denied. A socialist economy is inescapably dependent upon political mechanisms to allocate scarce resources, whereas a capitalist society offers an escape from politics through voluntary market exchange.

Shortly after the debate, Nutter shared a written transcript of his comments with William F. Buckley, indicating he would likely "toss them in the wastebasket" if the conservative editor of *National Review* could find no use for them.[6] Nutter's papers contain few clues as to why he changed his heart, but within a year's time he had expanded the transcript into a series of lectures on how the Soviet government treated its ordinary citizens. He delivered one version the following year at a conference for the American Bar Association.[7] At some point shortly thereafter, David Appel, a features

---

6 Nutter to Buckley. 1967. May 3. William F. Buckley Papers, Yale University.

7 Nutter, G. Warren. 1969. "Economic Aspects of Freedom," in Liberty under Law, Anarchy, Totalitarianism. American Bar Association, Standing Committee on Education About Communism.

editor at the *Philadelphia Inquirer*, approached the economist about developing the lectures into a multipart series on daily life in the Soviet Union. Nutter composed ten articles for the paper, drawing on the previous two decades of his research and developing its implications for Ivan Ivanov, a generic Soviet counterpart to the American John Doe. After the series ran in March 1968, he compiled its contents and edited them into the present manuscript.

The book's publication came shortly after Nutter accepted an appointment as assistant secretary for international security affairs in the Department of Defense. In part, the government appointment proved to be his own exit strategy from a devolving political climate at the University of Virginia. A few years prior, an increasingly hostile university administration began the systematic dismantling of the economics department after faculty in other departments deemed it overly "conservative." Coase had been chased away to the University of Chicago by a hostile dean who denigrated his academic work and impeded his promotion through the department. Buchanan left in protest the previous year after the university blocked the promotion of their widely published colleague Gordon Tullock. Nutter simply took a leave from his academic post and would return to the department after his service concluded, although the department was only a shadow of its most vibrant years in the late 1950s and early 1960s.

In a sense, *Ivan Ivanov* provided something of a final capstone for the broader scholarly project that emerged from the Thomas Jefferson Center during its heyday. In addition to the aforementioned faculty affiliates, this unique academic convergence had cultivated a generation of new scholars steeped in price theory, birthed the public choice subfield, and produced dozens of seminal works on economic theory and its political dimensions—Nutter's empirical analysis of the Soviet economy among them.

Though generally well-received in the Cold War environment of its publication, *Ivan Ivanov*, unfortunately, drifted from memory along with its own Soviet subject matter. In this new edition, we aim to make this text accessible again—both as a record of the daily personal hardships experienced under an actual Marxian-socialist state and a warning for a time when socialism's reputation has become detached from its own track record. The poverty, fear, and coerced subordination of Ivan Ivanov's life were not aberrations of a socialist revolution gone astray—they were the entirely predictable results of that same socialist system. And as its human toll stretches from the Eastern Bloc to China to Cuba to Venezuela, they continue to repeat with alarming certainty whenever and wherever socialism is attempted.

Phillip W. Magness

December 2019

I

I Choose Capitalism

May 3, 1967

Mr. William F. Buckley, Jr.

National Review

150 East 35th Street

New York, New York 10016

Dear Bill:

Last February I appeared in a debate with Herbert Aptheker at the University of Western Ontario, for which I prepared the enclosed

1

paper. I doubt that you go in for publishing old speeches, but I thought I would send it along to you in any case. If you have no use for it, send it back, and I will toss it in the wastebasket.

Best regards.

Sincerely yours,
G. Warren Nutter

GWN/mf
Enclosure

The history of mankind is in the main a dreary story of hunger, disease, despotism, and warfare—a constant struggle of man against the elements against himself. The blessings of democratic rule, liberty, tranquility, and material comfort have been enjoyed by only a tiny fraction of mankind over a tinier fraction of time and space.

Today on this continent one may, by crossing a single border, move from a country where the life expectancy is nearly 70 years to another whose it is close to 40. The contrast is, of course, greater in the case of more remote parts of the world, where the masses are normally one small step away from starvation.

Yet, poor or rich, men have never seemed to lack ambition to conquer, dominate, and oppress their fellow men. Any excuse will do, whether salvation, acculturation, or liberation. No lust is more obsessive or compulsive than that for power, and even the most humble of men may succumb to its seduction when he finds power thrust upon himself. We would do well to incant Lord Acton's dictum as a ritual: "Power corrupts; absolute power corrupts absolutely." And we might add: "The corrupt seek power; the absolutely corrupt seek absolute power."

Where progress has emerged from man's struggle through history, it has done so by virtue of a unique combination of circumstances that have, at once, dispersed power and channeled competitive drives into productive activity.

That unique combination of circumstances has come to be known as "capitalism."

I should perhaps pause here to record my attitude toward history, as a prelude to later comments about communism, the second half to our topic tonight. I cannot discern, as some do, grand design in history, and inexorable, predetermined course, either theological or scientific. The pronouncement of immutable historical laws strikes me as the ultimate in mysticism. Nor can I see history as a mere jumble of accidents—in the words of a famed historian, as "just one damned thing after another."

Chance and choice are both ingredients of history, together with no small amount of sheer momentum. History is made up of opportunities and constraints, and neither flow mechanically from the nature of man, conscious actions, ideology, customs, institutions, or any other easily identified source. History is instead the joint product of multifarious interacting forces, all mutually determining each other.

How does one explain the curious fact of history that Thomas Jefferson, James Madison, and James Monroe all come from the environs of Charlottesville, then a small village—even now a small town—in the foothills of Virginia, and since renowned primarily as their residence? Perhaps I am unduly impressed by this accident of history because my university is now in that small town.

But even more interesting is that strange confluence of thought that made the twelve months of 1776 mark the birth of a new concept of government, a science of economics, and a revolutionary technology. I speak of course of Thomas Jefferson's Declaration of Independence, Adam Smith's *Wealth of Nations*, and James Watts' steam engine.

However accidental this confluence, it was not by chance that these three streams, natural complements of each other, mingled so well together. Having joined together, they brought to man in our part of the world more progress toward freedom, justice, and prosperity within the span of a few generations than had been enjoyed over all ages before. They carved a grand oasis in the sands of history.

But that very progress, with its revolutionary impact, shook loose the age-old endurance that man has customarily displayed toward his lot, and read in its place an attitude of unending discontent with the pace at which remaining problems were being met. And so we now find ourselves in a society where progress and discontent are in a race with each other.

This is as it should be as long as there is poverty and injustice in the midst of plenty. If social change is to move in the right direction, in accord with the standards of the civilized world, there must always be those who stir and prod, who keep the public alert to inequities, who find fault with established ways of maintaining social order. It is natural to point the finger of blame at the existing system and to seek salvation in its opposite, and therein lies the great danger of our day.

Those who protest against the failures of capitalism, real and imagined, too often see their remedy in turning things over to government, in expanding the political order and contracting the economic—more accurately, the area of voluntary association. Of course, political action is often the preferable route and sometimes the necessary one. But not always or even most of the time. The danger we run in looking first to government to solve problems is that progress will grind to a halt—that discontent will vanquish progress, and the race will be over.

Perhaps it is well to recall that the bane of progress over the history of mankind has been too much government, not too little. The documents of 1776 protested against too much government, not against too little. And liberty came to have the specific meaning of freedom from government, from arbitrary power, from paternalistic rule.

Progress came with the loosening of political bonds, and the replacement of commands by voluntary exchange in the marketplace. Private property is simply the other side of the coin to liberty. It is the means, and pragmatically the only means, whereby power may be dispersed within a society. In the absolute state, private property vanishes by being concentrated solely in the hands of the ruler. The pharoah of ancient Egypt quite literally owned everybody and everything; he could do with them as he pleased. The tsars of Russia made the same claim with perhaps less success, while Stalin succeeded without the same claim.

It is clear to me that no society can exist in which everything is privately owned, because there must always be government—a political order—representing, in one manner or another, the collectivity. There will therefore always be collective property in the form of the power of the state. The taxing power is, after all, the most obvious property right of government.

It is equally clear to me that no society can be free or democratic, in the true meaning of those words, unless property is broadly dispersed and predominantly private. Let me be quite specific: I see no possibility of the "democratic socialism" if both words are to be taken literally. It is, in my opinion, no historical accident that democracy, individual freedom, and capitalism have gone hand in hand.

To avoid any misunderstanding that may be creeping into your minds, let me assure you that I do not intend to spend my few minutes here eulogizing capitalism with a capital "C"—or any other ism, for that matter. No system is absolutely good under any and all circumstances or in any and all respects, just as no system is immutably fixed in any mind, scripture, or set of institutions. Many features of the capitalist system, in both philosophical and institutional forms, are repugnant to me, and I would support some other order if I could only have power at the same time to remake the world and the people inhabiting it. I have at least as many complaints against capitalism as I do against the weather.

But we must choose between feasible alternatives in this world, and not between utopias. The capitalist order, as it has evolved, is the least bad one I know, and it is the order most susceptible and amenable to reform improvement.

The paramount virtue of capitalism is that it fosters progress through diversity and freedom without sacrificing efficiency, justice, and charity. One can be even stronger: it is also more efficient, more just, more charitable, and more egalitarian than any other viable system. Provided only that there is effective dispersal of power and property, the capitalist order is driven by competition in manifold ways in the field of ideas as well as commodities. The competitive marketplace, in its broadest sense, is the most potent guardian we have against authoritarianism and all that it implies. In a truly competitive society, there cannot be a single gospel, a single scripture, or a single priesthood to interpret them.

In my few moments tonight, I can do no more than touch on these points. A tedious sermon on the workings of a capitalist system would no doubt be a colossal bore in any case, merely repeating commonplaces. Perhaps I can perform my duty better by turning directly to the task of comparing communism and capitalism.

Communism is at once a set of doctrines and a set of concrete institutions, and both are subject to continual mutation and alteration. The ideology as it derives from Marx and his various recognized disciples is as much negative as positive, consisting as it does in an indictment of capitalism. Indeed, Marx is largely silent on the nature of the new order that is to emerge when capitalism destroys itself through his historical law of contradiction. Since government is the creature of the capitalist class, it too will wither away and be replaced by a harmonious anarchy. And so on.

Marx is quite explicit in his predictions of the concrete working out of this inexorable historical process. Exploitation of the masses, he says, follows directly from the implicit division of society into two classes: the privileged few who own property—the capitalists—and the downtrodden masses who do not—the proletariat. But "them as has, gets," so that property must become progressively more concentrated, business progressively more monopolistic, and the working class progressively more miserable.

Now, one can flatly state that none of these predictions has come true in any major capitalist country. As national income has risen beyond the imagination of an earlier age, it has become more, not less, evenly distributed. The worker's standard of living has risen more than apace. And there has been absolutely no evidence of a decline in competition. On the contrary, the evidence points strongly toward an increase. On this matter, I speak with conviction, since I have studied the evidence carefully.

Yet we must give Marx his due. Surely there is nothing in capitalism in and of itself that guarantees a dispersed and just distribution of property or a generally competitive environment, and those who try to argue otherwise harm their cause. The historical record is in important part the result of conscious political policies designed to alter the economic environment, polices quite consistent in the main with a predominantly capitalist system. I speak here of such things as antitrust legislation, subsidized education, income and inheritance taxation, and so on and on.

Other forces have also been important. Of course, luck plays a major role in how well one is endowed with those qualities valued by his society: brains, cunning, beauty, at times ugliness, material wealth—in sum, anything rare relative to the demand for it. Effort also plays a role. And from one generation to another, the distribution of luck and effort varies, so that some fortunes may vanish and others accumulate. Simultaneously, the competitive process generates perpetual innovation, destroying old property and creating new.

Within the ecological equilibrium of the economy as it moves over time, many things are being born, many maturing, many decaying, and many dying.

Compare, if you will, the environment in societies that embody communism in its institutional form. Without exception, communist societies have been monistic and authoritarian, while capitalist societies are typically, though not always, pluralistic and liberal. There is one Truth and one Truth alone in a communist country, and its source is the communist scriptures as interpreted by the leaders of the self-appointed elite. What is the fate of the dissenter or the member of a minority—of minorities themselves? Where are the forces of diverse experimentation and innovation? Where is freedom, equality or justice?

There is the apocryphal story of the Soviet political commentator who, on being asked to describe the difference between capitalism and communism, replied: "As you know, capitalism is the exploitation of man by man. Well, communism is the precise opposite."

In the Soviet Union, tyranny and conquest are justified in the name of the scientific laws of communism, just as they were in old Russia in the name of the divine right of the tsars. In many respects but with important qualifications, communism has become throughout the world a little more than the modern rationalization for arbitrary power, and this is precisely why would-be dictators everywhere have been so easily brought into the communist camp. The major communist powers constitute themselves the grand protectors of lesser dictatorial regimes in exchange for feudal allegiance, in much the ancient way.

If I may digress for a moment, I would say that I view the Russian communist revolution, now approaching its fiftieth year, as one of the great reactionary events of all time. As I read the history of tsarist Russia, it is the story of a slow and tortuous movement over the centuries away from oriental despotism toward a liberal order in the Western tradition. Reform of the system accelerated in the last half of the nineteenth century and the first decades of the twentieth, reaching a climax with the constitutional revolution of February 1917. But the bolshevik coup of October and its ultimate aftermath threw the country back to conditions of despotism, terror, and serfdom unsurpassed under the worst of the tsars—all in the name of "construction of socialism." The slow and tortuous movement toward liberalism continues to assert itself beneath all the turmoil, and we may perhaps expect the reactions to be overcome eventually. But I venture that this will not happen unless capitalistic institutions gradually infiltrate the society.

To return to the main thread, let me briefly explore the plight of minority groups under communism and capitalism. I speak here with some authority and experience since I seem to have been in some minority or other as long as I can remember—religiously, ethnically, academically, politically, or what have you.

Minorities suffer in every society simply because they differ from the dominant group in some way considered significant and undesirable. They are, in the current phrase, discriminated against, and the roots of such discrimination lie in concrete personal attitudes of members of the dominant group, not in some abstract mentality of some abstract collectivity. Discrimination may be practiced privately or collectively, and the latter is always more effective and harmful than the former. In any event, it is vain to expect private manifestations of prejudice to vanish until we enter a golden age of angels on earth. In the world of practical alternatives, the important question to raise in judging a society is whether there are means whereby minorities may escape the rigors of collective discrimination, coercively enforced.

The case of the Negro in my own country immediately comes to mind. Every one who believes in a civilized and humane society must condemn the coercive segregation of Negroes enforced by law over so many years in various parts of the United States. One can only applaud the removal of those barriers and press for continued elimination of all discriminatory treatment under the law. One must also deplore unfair discrimination in private affairs and attempt to reduce it through persuasion while recognizing that it can weaken only with the passage of time.

At the same time, one can imagine how much worse conditions would be, and would have been, for the Negro were it not for the primarily competitive market. On this point, I need only quote and endorse what the eminent economist, Milton Friedman has said:

It is a striking historical fact that the development of capital-ism has been accompanied by a major reduction in the extent to which particular religious, racial, or social groups have operated under special handicaps in respect of their economic activities; have, as the saying goes, been discriminated against. The substitution of contract arrangements for status arrange-ments was the first step toward the freeing of the serfs in the Middle Ages. The preservation of Jews through the Middles Ages was possible because of the existence of a market sector in which they could operate and maintain themselves despite official persecution. Puritans and Quakers were able to migrate to the New World because they could accumulate the funds to do so in the market despite disabilities imposed on them in other aspects of their life. The Southern states after the Civil War took many measures to impose legal restrictions on Negroes. One measure which was never taken on any scale was the establishment of barriers to the ownerships of either real or personal property. The failure to impose such barriers clearly did not reflect any special concern to avoid restrictions on Negroes. It reflected rather, a basic belief in private property which was so strong that it overrode the desire to discriminate against Negroes. The maintenance of the general rules of private property and of capitalism have been a major source of opportunity for Negroes and have permitted them to make greater progress than they otherwise would have made. To take a more general example, the reserves of discrimination in any society are the areas that are most monopolistic in character, whereas discrimination against groups of particuluar color or religion is least in those areas where there is the greatest freedom of compeition.[8]

As an aside, let me say that the single most pernicious anti-Negro legislation on our books today is the minimum wage law, precisely because it bars so many of them from the escape route of the market.

Now ask yourselves how a similar minority fares in a communist country with its authoritairan rule, and you will find the answer in the treatment of many such groups in the Soviet Union: the Jews, Jehovah's Witnesses, the gypsies, the Kazakhs, the Crimean Tatars, the Volga Germans,—in brief, every nonconformist group. Where can these groups turn to escape persecution by the all-powerful state? Only to the weak and generally illicit marketplaces.

This leads me to the final major point I wish to make tonight. Without exception communist countries have gone as far as possible

8 Friedman, M. 1962. *Capitalism and Freedom*. The University of Chicago Press, 108-109.

in eliminating the market from their economics, substituting instead a system of administrative planning, control, and management. The price they have paid is gross inefficiency as well as loss of freedom.

Let me illustrate the choice they have made by reciting Michael Polanyi's parable of the sack of potatoes. Suppose you have a sack of potatoes and wish to make it as compact as possible. One way is to measure the configureation of every potato and try to fit it in its optimum palce in the sack so that all potatoes together take up the least possible room. You might do this by trial and error or by feeding your measurements into computer programmed to work out the answer. Any competent mathematician will tell you, however, that this problem is beyond solution by the most powerful computers known, and ceratinly no general rules for arranging potatoes can be worked out that will apply to all possible sackfuls.

Another way to solve the problem is to lift the sack and give it a couple of shakes.

A moment's reflection will tell you that the market is a marvelous, automatic mechanism for shaking millions of sacks of potatoes. I need not remind you that communist countires are now trying to find more and more ways of using the market in place of central-ized administrative planning. Here I will let a prominent Soviet economist, Professor Aganbegian, speak for himself:

The seven-year plan has failed. Not only that, but with the

end of the first ten-year part of our twenty-year plan none of the quotas have been attained…

There has not…been any rise in the standard of living during recent years. Ten million people have suffered a decrease in their living standards…

Our systems of planning, establishing incentives, and managing industry were developed in the 1930's. Ever since then nothing has changed except the names given things, but in fact everything remained based on the administrative methods of planning and management. The extreme centralization and the absecnce of economic democracy have a very serious effect on our economy…

As a matter of fact our prices and our monetary value relationships serve no purpose at all. The thing most imporant is centralized distribution…

The national plan is in no sense [equilibrated], and it would be impossible to [equilibrate] it because that would require balancing 4,000 different items against one another. Nor is the plan [equilibrated] in even its essential elements because, if it were, then one could not achieve some goals without achieving others; [to attempt such an integrated program] would cause a breakdown of the whole economy, so in fact this is not done...[9]

Let me conclude on this note: the communist world is in a state of flux, ideologically, economically, and politically. The Soviet empire seems to be disintegrating, the communist economies are passing through a crisis of decision, and great upheavals are underway in countries like China. With typical irony, the Poles have developed the saying: "Under communism, only the future is certain; the past is always changing."

Given this state of flux, what one has to say today about the two great systems, capitalism and communism, may not hold tomorrow. And surely one must focus on far more than differences in material achievements.

The greatness of society does not come from its monuments but from the kind of people it produces. Justice, responsibility, and humanity—these are the qualities of greatness in a people. Only the humane can remain free, and only the free can remain humane.

It is for this reason that I choose capitalism.

---

9 ASTE Bulletin. 1965. Summer, 1–4.

Needless to say, this speech was not published in the Soviet Union. The purported text was first published in Italian in the July 1965 issue of *Bandiera Rossa*, a Trotskyite journal printed in Rome. There are persuasive reasons for believing the text to be genuine.

June 1, 1967

Dear Warren:

Thanks so much for sending me your eloquent speech. It was of course wasted on Herbert Aptheker, but you weren't addressing him—you were addressing the students. I'd be interested in its effectivness. I think you hit just the right tone. Again my congratulations and thanks.

As ever,
Wm. F. Buckley, Jr.

Mr. G. Warren Nutter
University of Virginia
James Wilson Department of Economics
Rouss Hall
Charlottesville, Virginia 22903

II

The Bulwarks of Liberty

In September 1965, two prominent Russian authors, Andrei Sinyavsky and Yuli Daniel, were quietly put under arrest. Five months later they were brought to trial in the glare of publicity, convicted after four days of testimony, and sentenced to seven and five years' imprisonment, respectively. Their crime: publishing literary works abroad that, in the eyes of their country's rulers, derogated and defamed the motherland.

Soviet citizens are not forbidden by law to publish their writings in foreign lands or to use pen names, as these two authors did. And so they were charged instead with sedition and subversion, a strange accusation since their words did not reach the eyes of their countrymen. Yet we must become accustomed to the strange in trying to discern substance from form in Soviet society.

The constitution of the Soviet Union promises to every citizen freedom of speech, press, assembly, and religious worship. The words are familiar, but their meaning is not. Freedom of expression, the constitution states, is guaranteed "in conformity with the interests of the working people, and in order to strengthen the socialist system."[10] In principle, this clause has been interpreted to mean that a person may speak his mind as long as he intends no disrespect for the existing order or causes no harm to it. In practice, the restrictions on free expression are even more severe.

Democracy means, more than anything else, government by discussion. In our society, one needs only a soapbox and a corner or a duplicating machine and paper to make his views heard in the constant discourse that evolves into public policy. Of course, free speech does not give one the right to shout "Fire!" in a crowded theater, as Justice Oliver Wendell Holmes reminded us. But on political matters, freedom of expression cannot be abridged unless there is a clear and present danger of the violent overthrow of our form of government.

There are limits to what John Doe may say and how he may say it if he is to avoid penalties, but the limits are carefully prescribed

---

10 Soviet Constitution in Hazard. 1964. *The Soviet System of Government.* Chicago: University of Chicago Press, 241.

by law. First of all, he must conform to the laws governing slander, libel, fraud, and obscenity. The purpose of these restrictions is to prevent unjust injury to other individuals, not to the state. We adhere to the firm principle that no one is entitled to further his own interests by harming others.

Secondly, John Doe must not incite public disorder. If he harangues a mob to the point of violence, he is as guilty as the rioters themselves. He must be presumed to be aware of the natural consequences of his acts, and he does not have the right to speak for the purpose of endangering public safety. We know from the long history of mankind that otherwise responsible and rational individuals may lose control of their passions when they are members of a mob. Here the concept of injury embraces damage not only to individuals but also to just and orderly processes of social relations.

Finally, John Doe must respect the security of his country. He is not free to divulge secrets that he knows are vital to national security, or to agitate for mutiny and insurrection. In time of war, further restrictions are imposed because the survival of a democratic society is at stake.

There is always the danger that these exceptions may serve as excuses for steady encroachment on the freedom of expression, and there is no magic safeguard to prevent this from happening. Ultimately, we rely on our heritage, our institutions, and our individual conscience to protect our freedoms. Beyond that, "The price of liberty is eternal vigilance."

We have been fortunate, for the exceptions remain just that. No person in the United States needs to fear imprisonment for expression of his political beliefs. It is no crime even to advocate the overthrow of the government. It is quite common for a worker to disagree with the politics of his boss and say so openly, or for professional colleagues to make a display of political disagreement. Vigorous debate is a common place. Indeed it is the means whereby a minority has the opportunity for persuading the majority to adopt its opinions. At the bottom is a rejection of the principle of truth by authority, the principle that truth depends on who says it. Our form of government stands on the contrary principle of truth by agreement, everyone having an opportunity to persuade others of their errors.

Not so in the Soviet Union. There the Communist Party is the sole arbiter of what is right or wrong, what is true or false. It is so as a matter of both ideology and power.

When those who run a country consider themselves infallible, they may be expected to view all dissenters as troublemakers and traitors. Some are merely declared insane and committed to asylums. Others are treated more harshly. When the state owns and runs virtually everything, a worker cannot even complain about the conditions of work, no matter how harmlessly, without running the risk of being charged with disloyalty. To offer constructive criticism of the way affairs are managed if only in a local plant or on a farm, is to attack an organ of the state.

Not even members of parliament dare to oppose decisions openly. Not a single act of legislation has ever been passed except by unanimous vote. If the presumed representatives of the people are afraid to open their mouths, what can one expect of the man in the street?

Those who grow up under such a system soon become wary of expressing their thoughts in an unknown company. They know that detailed files are collected by the secret police on persons suspected of being unfriendly to the regime. They know that informers abound in the form of professional agents of the control apparatus, dedicated Party members, and sheer opportunists. A lively conversation among close friends is likely to stop or turn to trivialities when a stranger enters the room. Academics at scientific meetings in foreign lands must be cautious about what they say since every delegation has at least one member who serves as the ear of the Party.

Privacy is an elusive luxury for most Russians. It is sometimes most easily found on crowded streets or in noisy public places. They expect as a matter of course that their mail will be read, their phones tapped, and their meeting places bugged. Their rulers recognize no communications are privileged, not even those between parishioner and pastor, accused and legal counsel, or husband and wife. There is no region of personal confidence in which the state may not intrude as a self-asserted right.

The average Russian family—let us call it the Ivanov family—lives in crowded conditions, very often a single room. It is not unknown in the cities to find two related families sharing the same room, separating themselves by curtains or other makeshift barriers. The government assigns living quarters, and ordinary individuals and families have no choice over who will live in other rooms in the same apartment. Each family must share bathroom and kitchen facilities with others unless the head of the household belongs to a privileged class.

The contrast with our society is clear. We enjoy and cherish the right to privacy because it is inherent and essential in our system of government. We believe that every competent and mature individual is the best judge of his own welfare, that he should live his own life and pursue his own happiness, and that he is normally the best guardian of his children's welfare.

This is indeed the ultimate meaning of liberty and the justification for it. Liberty basically means freedom from the government. The government is designed to serve the individual by preserving his privacy and preventing others from infringing on his rights. In addition to safeguarding life, limb, and property, the government takes on the positive role—difficult and large enough to keep it well occupied—of promoting equality of opportunity and serving as guardian for the incompetent and unfortunate.

Reasonable men will differ on how far the ranges of individual freedom and collective or governmental action should extend in the lives of citizens, and we witness intense controversy on this question in the political arena of our country today. Yet there remains a deep consensus on the right to privacy and widespread concern for its preservation in the face of threats posed by the growth of government and technological advances in the art of eavesdropping.

The threats are real enough. In the age of computers with incredible capacities for storing and retrieving information, it is no longer an idle thought that the central government could collect an accessible file of intimate details on every citizen, whether those details are a matter of legitimate concern to the government or not. Wires no longer need to be tapped to record conversations. Recording may be done by electronic means, even at a great distance from where the words are being spoken and with devices impossible to detect.

Loss of privacy is the first step toward entrenchment of arbitrary government, and our courts seem to be aware of that fact as they search for safeguards against unbridled snooping by government. The courts remain firm in barring privileged communications and information improperly obtained—through invasion of privacy—as evidence in court. Congress shows similar concern in restricting the recordkeeping authority of the executive branch.

It is the bitter lesson of history that society cannot rely on the scruples of a powerful ruler to restrain him from exercising his power over the lives of his subjects. The only safeguard of liberty is the restraint of power itself.

The rights to privacy and free speech are important restraints of arbitrary power. And the individual voice may be amplified many-fold by the printing press. For this reason George Mason, in his declaration of rights adopted by the state of Virginia in 1776, spoke of freedom of the press as ''one of the great bulwarks of liberty.''

In this country, there are hundreds of independent printers and publishers engaged in the business of printing and disseminating ideas. Anybody with something to say that can command even a moderate audience can be assured of finding someone who will publish his words.

Failing all else, John Doe may buy, rent, or borrow a mimeograph machine to reproduce his tracts and distribute them—provided they are not obscene, fraudulent, or libelous—on street corners or through the mails to whatever audience he can muster. Everybody's free to compete in the marketplace for ideas, at a profit to himself if they are widely received, possibly at some expense if they are not. Of course, it is impossible to guarantee that whatever anyone might wish to put in print will find ready readers, but at least in our society nobody is prevented from making the effort.

In the Soviet Union, the constitutional guarantee of a free press is a mere figment. Every printing establishment employing labor must be owned by the state, and every private firm consisting solely of the owner is specifically forbidden to operate any equipment designed for reproduction, even the simplest duplicating machine. Everybody is therefore dependent on the pleasure of the government for publication of his writings.

Moreover, an independent censoring agency must examine all manuscripts and approve of them in advance before they may be published. And though the work was originally passed by the censor, it may later be declared undesirable and removed from circulation. And so books are burned as well as banned. Once a published book has been officially condemned, it is not altogether wise for Ivan to keep a copy on his bookshelves.

The typical Russian is an avid reader of any good literature he can get his hands on, poetry as well as prose. Ivan may go to the government bookstore and purchase ample volumes of Russian classics at low prices. He may find even more literature written in the style of so-called "socialist realism," but he is less likely to be interested in it. There will be books of some American authors— mainly social critics like Mark Twain, Theodore Dreiser, Jack London, and John Steinbeck—translated into Russian. Ivan may keep up with recent trends in literature by reading some of the literary journals.

Communist doctrine asserts, of course, that its system provides far more freedom of expression than ours. According to this doctrine, the Communist government is merely the custodian of the interests of the toiling masses, and as such is fully responsive to their will. If no dissent from the official line appears in print, that is because there is none. After all, political differences arise only out of the class struggle, which has virtually disappeared in the Soviet Union, along with vestiges of capitalism.

In the United States, on the other hand, so the doctrine goes, all publication is controlled by the monopoly capitalists who own the printing presses. The dominant capitalist class can make sure no views unfriendly to its interests appear in print. If some should by chance slip through, they will be rendered harmless by being denied channels of dissemination and by being discredited in the media of mass communication, which are firmly under the control of a few wealthy families.

We must wait to dispel the fallacies in this doctrine one by one. For the moment it is sufficient to say that the picture of Soviet life as a state of blissful relations between the masses and their government is grotesquely distorted, just as is the vision of the United States as a country dominated by a handful of billionaire capitalists.

It is true that the system of mass communication in the United States could stand improvement. Few of our cities are served by more than two independent newspapers, and many by only one. There are only three major networks in television and only four in radio. Three firms dominate the field of weekly news magazines.

Yet John Doe has at his disposal enormously varied sources of news and opinions if he exerts the slightest effort. He need not be the captive of his local newspaper. There are always others available, some with nationwide and others with regional distribution. John may tune in to local radio stations all over the country and in foreign lands as well. Within areas of moderately concentrated population, he may watch at least half a dozen television stations.

There are countless journals of opinion, large and small, commercial and nonprofit, partisan and nonpartisan. At a small expense of time and funds, he may read the views of many diverse factions of organized labor, trade associations, political parties, professions, and other special interests.

Commentators of almost all shades of opinion offer their interpretations of the news. John can find out what Communists of both domestic and foreign varieties have to say in easily accessible newspapers, journals, books, and radio programs. Whatever materials he may not wish or be able to purchase for himself may be borrowed from public and educational libraries.

In short, there are few important barriers except time and effort to prevent an American from becoming fully informed on the boundless variety of beliefs, opinions, and interpretations prevailing in the world at large.

Contrast this with the situation in the Soviet Union. All publishing activities are firmly under the control of the Party and government, from censoring to printing to distributing. Every bookstore, library, and newsstand is owned by the state. No printed materials, particularly from abroad, may be distributed in any way, whether sold or given away, except through state channels. A number of foreigners have been imprisoned for the innocent crime of handing out foreign literature, a seditious activity in the eyes of Soviet law.

The state has a complete monopoly on all media of mass communication. There are two sets of newspapers, one published by the Party and the other by the government. The major newspaper of the Party is *Pravda*, or "truth," and that of the government is *Izvestia*, or "news." But, as the saying goes, there is little truth in the one and little news in the other. Both are published in Moscow, and they have counterparts in other localities.

For Americans accustomed to reading a daily newspaper with two dozen or more pages and an even larger Sunday edition, it is difficult to imagine the sparse diet of the news fed to the ordinary Russian. The standard size of *Pravda* is six pages, no matter what the day of the week.

When Ivan takes his daily *Pravda* in hand, he expects to be greeted on the front page with the usual editorial praising socialism or exhorting the populace to greater effort. He is also bound to find a prominent article describing a great victory on the economic front. Party resolutions, governmental decrees, and similar announcements occupy most of the remaining space. In the lower right-hand corner, he may discover some brief news items.

The second page is normally devoted to larger doses of propaganda. If some special event has taken place, such as a Party Congress or meeting of the Parliament, he will have to content himself with a newspaper full of speeches. Since his rulers have the habit of speaking from four to six hours at a time, it will take a lot of space to report what they have said. Only on the last page or two can Ivan hope to find more news flashes, a brief report on sports, and the schedule of radio and television programs.

Until recent years, the Soviet Union was sealed off from the outside world by an almost impenetrable electronic as well as paper curtain. Virtually all broadcasts except music were obliterated by an elaborate jamming network. Now the jamming is less extensive, but it is still used to prevent objectionable programs from reaching Russian ears. The state exercises a complete monopoly over broadcasting within Soviet boundaries and allows only certain types of receiving equipment to be used.

Ultimate control over the press and airways is exercised by the central core of the Communist Party through general policy directives and specific orders, issued whenever the occasion arises. Control cannot be perfect or complete in such a large country, but in most important respects everything that is printed or broadcast conforms to the Party line. At the same time, there is room for interpretation, and an energetic editor, particularly of a literary journal, may take advantage of it to experiment with works of less conventional form and content. An outstanding example in recent years has been the literary magazine *Novy Mir*.

It would be incorrect to presume that the press contains nothing but uncritical adulation of Soviet society. Organized campaigns to overcome problems are often officially launched in which some flaw under attack is subjected to harsh criticism. Normally such words are reserved for "the bureaucracy," some faltering sector of the economy, the managerial staff of an inefficient enterprise, or assorted "enemies of the people." Both in the midst of such campaigns and at other appropriate times, similar criticisms may be published in the form of letters to the editor or satirical cartoons. There is even a special humor magazine for this purpose, called *Krokodil*.

What is unheard of is any hint of the disapproval of policies laid down by any political organ of the state, any question about the conduct or decisions of political leaders, or any doubts about the virtues of Communism or the wickedness of capitalism. A Russian Al Capp or Art Buchwald is unthinkable.

Under Communism, the Poles are fond of saying, only the future is certain: The past is always changing. Hence it is not unusual to find that leaders formerly praised as immortal heroes may be revealed when they have died, like Stalin, or been deposed, like Khrushchev. But this is not for the individual to decide. The highest Party authority formulates and lays down the line. Those who wish to keep out of trouble follow it.

On this score, an official series of movies was released late in 1967 covering each of the fifty years of Soviet rule. Stalin appeared once in a while in those on his era, usually without comment. However, many of the policies of that period were denounced. In contrast, Khrushchev was not mentioned once by name in the films shown on the years of his rule, and he did not appear in recognizable form. Nikita has become an Orwellian unperson.

Freedom as we know it is foreign to the typical resident of the Soviet Union. In this respect, life has been even bleaker over much of the Soviet era than it is today. The Russian, whose culture has been shaped by centuries of despotism, has a remarkable capacity for enduring physical and spiritual hardship. Yet he, like every human being, has the spark of liberty in his breast.

And so we witness today an uneasy stir in the land, a malaise and dissatisfaction that may one day burst forth into a sustained cry for reform and freedom. Spokesmen for the cause of freedom are emerging among the intellectuals on whom so much educational effort has been spent. In their vanguard, as is so often the case, stand poets, artists, and writers. Sinyavsky and Daniel have made their sacrifice, and others are likely to follow. Some of the most courageous and moving words of protest are those of Lidiya Chukovskaya, a respected literary figure, and daughter of a renowned author. In an open letter addressed to Mikhail Sholokhov, the Russian Nobel laureate who supported the action against Sinyavsky and Daniel and found their treatment too lenient, she wrote:

> On the surface, the trial of Siniyavsky and Daniel was held
> with due regard to the legal formalities. For you, this is a fault,
> and for me, it is a good feature. Yet, even so, I protest against
> the sentence pronounced by the court.
>
> Why?
>
> Because Sinyavsky and Daniel's committal to trial was in
> itself illegal.
>
> Because a book, a piece of fiction, a story, a novel, in brief,
> a work of literature—whether good or bad, talented or untal-
> ented, truthful or untruthful—cannot be tried by a criminal
> court. Ideas should be fought with ideas, not with camps and
> prisons.
>
> This is what you should have said to your listeners if you had
> really gone to the rostrum as a spokesman of Soviet literature.
>
> But your spoke as a renegade from it. Your shameful speech
> will not be forgotten by history.
>
> And literature will take its own vengeance, as it always
> takes vengeance on those who betray the duty imposed on it.
> It has condemned you to the worst sentence to which an artist
> can be condemned—to creative sterility. And neither honors
> nor money nor prizes, given at home or abroad, can turn this

shame from your head.[11]

This stirring protest and others like it have evoked a response from the state in the form of stern efforts to tighten, not loosen, thought control. New laws extend the penalties for disseminating "recognizably false fabrications defaming the Soviet state and social order," for organizing or participating in demonstrations, and for displaying contempt for the Soviet flag.

The four young writers who so bravely sent to the outside world a transcript of the Sinyavsky-Daniel trial were convicted in January 1968 of a crime against the state. The two principals received sentences as severe as those imposed on Sinyavsky and Daniel. The courageous voice of Pavel Litvinov, grandson of the late Maxim Litvinov, once Soviet foreign minister, still speaks out against these injustices, but one may wonder for how long. He has already been dismissed from his post as a lecturer in physics, and arrest may be imminent.

We must wait to see who will win this tragic struggle for more freedom and when.

---

11 Chukovskaya letter in *The New York Times*. 1966. Nov. 19, 6.

III

Peaceable Assembly

In the Soviet Union, any crowd that gathers for any purpose without prior official permission is subject to criminal prosecution. Under Soviet law, two persons are a crowd.

No society can be democratic unless the people have the right to translate their ideas into action by peaceably assembling together. In our country, any group that wishes to convene may, as an inalienable right, do so at its pleasure. Any group that wishes to demonstrate in order to influence the views of others, or to petition for a redress of grievances, is guaranteed the right to do so, subject only to regulations required to maintain public order.

We witness today the inviolable nature of this right in the

demonstrations organized against the draft and the war in Vietnam. We witness it in orderly protest marches on behalf of civil rights. Scarcely a day goes by that some individual or group does not walk before the White House, displaying a message of grievance or persuasion.

The right to assemble does not, of course, convey a right to legislate in the streets by mob rule. If our democratic society is to flourish, laws must be enacted solely through the orderly processes provided by the Constitution. Everyone has the right to criticize any law and to urge its repeal, but no one has the right to break the law with impunity merely because he does not approve of it. Our system requires that existing law is respected while it is being subjected to constant scrutiny and change.

When a group commits an overt act after congregating for the purpose of defying or violating the law, its members have engaged in a criminal conspiracy and may be so prosecuted. Their proper course of action is to demonstrate and agitate peaceably, in conformance with the law, for the purpose of inspiring a redress of grievances through legislation or judicial decision.

Groups may at times be formed to engage in "civil disobedience," or deliberate violation of a specific civil law, in order to draw attention to the injustice that the violators see in it. They expect to suffer the penalty for breaking the law and usually will do so. Whether morally justified or not, civil disobedience has a very definite meaning and should not be used to describe other kinds of unlawful conduct.

Suppose, for instance, that law forbids Caucasians from riding in taxi cabs driven by Negroes, and vice versa. Let us ignore the question, by no means academic, of how Caucasians and Negroes are to be distinguished. It is an act of peaceable assembly to petition for a redress of grievances if a group gathers before the city hall with placards requesting repeal of this law. It is an act of civil disobedience for a group of Caucasians to hail a taxi driven by a Negro or for a group of Negroes to hail a taxi driven by a Caucasian. It is a conspiratorial and criminal act wholly unrelated to civil disobedience for a group to join together as a mob to disrupt traffic or to instigate a riot as a protest against this law.

Ours is a society of voluntary associations. John Doe, if he is a working man, may join with his fellow workers in forming a labor union, through which they will negotiate with their employer on various matters. For the pleasure of his leisure hours, he may belong to some lodge or club. In contributing to his favorite charities, he associates with others voluntarily to help the less fortunate.

When he uses his savings to purchase shares of stock in a business firm, he engages with others in a joint enterprise. He and his wife may come together with other parents and their children's teachers to form a local parent-teacher association. His children may join with others in and out of school to form clubs and similar groups of endless variety.

Mary Doe, depending on her leisure time and tastes, may join a bridge or sewing club, the women's auxiliary of a lodge, the voluntary aid service of a hospital or other charitable organization, the local League of Women Voters, and so on. The adult members of a family may become active members of a political party, and the teen-agers may participate in one of the party's affiliated organizations. The family may join an existing church or, with others of like belief, form their own congregation.

In all cases, these voluntary associations have an existence of their own and foster the purposes for which they were formed. From time to time the membership will be convened, and those who wish to attend the meetings may freely discuss affairs and participate in formulating policies. No one is compelled to belong or not belong to an organization, or to attend or not attend its meetings.

One is bound to find it difficult to appreciate the totally different environment in which the ordinary person finds himself in the Soviet Union. No association of individuals may be formed without an explicit license to do so from the state, and once formed the association must have a license for each meeting it plans to hold. In fact, no group may legally convene for any purpose, indoors or out, without a special license to do so. If people from different parts of the country are to congregate, approval must come directly from the Council of Ministers of the Soviet Union.

It is easy to see that our ordinary Russian, Ivan Ivanov, does not expect to participate in group activities except as they may be officially sponsored. "Social organizations" are created - and abolished - by the state from time to time, but there is never more than one of a kind in existence at any particular moment.

If Ivan and his wife, Anna, are workers, they will automatically become members of the trade union assigned to their place of work. As an arm of the government, the trade union may provide them with recreational and holiday facilities, but it will offer no services in the form of negotiations with their employers about wages or other conditions of work. Ivan cannot contemplate joining with other workers in a strike, for that would be a serious crime against the state. Nor does he expect to have any voice in the selection of officers and in other union affairs.

The prohibition against voluntary association extends to recreational and charitable activities for that matter, to every aspect of life. Needless to say, the formation of a business enterprise is out of the question.

If, along with half the population, the Ivanovs live in a rural community, they may technically be members of a so-called farming cooperative. But they are well aware through long experience that they have no say in management. When they are called to a meeting along with other members of the collective farm, they know they will be either given orders, exhorted to toil more arduously, or asked to confirm a farm manager already appointed by the authorities. Only rarely will they venture to utter anything but approving words, for they recognize the danger of being suspected as dissident and disloyal.

The Ivanovs will not dream of participating in political activities unless they are, through zeal and diligence, members of the small elite that forms the Communist Party and its affiliates. Candidates and members of the Communist Party itself are admitted through a rigorous selection policy and number fewer than thirteen million, or about one out of every ten adults in the Soviet Union. If Ivan is a member of the Party, he enjoys the privilege of airing some opinions at Party meetings, but he must do so as an individual. Party rules forbid the formation of factions for any purpose.

Every authorized organization and the very government itself is run by a core of Party members within it. This precaution ensures the conformity of all group activities with a single set of objectives and policies. There are and can be no competing or rival groups either in any sphere of life or among the various spheres.

Since the vast majority of Soviet citizens live their lives without any regard to politics, our representative family must be expected to do so as well. Even so, their school-age children will be enrolled as a matter of course in the Pioneers or, in the case of those under ten, the Little Octobrists. It is through these Party organizations that school children participate in group recreational activities and receive extensive political indoctrination.

When a child reaches the age of fifteen, he may apply for membership in the Young Communist League where his activities will take on much more of a political color. About forty percent of those in the eligible age groups join the Young Communists. Since one's career may be furthered by political activities, many of those who join may be motivated by opportunism rather than dedication.

Only the courageous will dare to form groups outside the official circle in defiance of the law. Only the most courageous groups will sign petitions or stage demonstrations. Despite the danger and the severity of punishment, protest meetings against such measures as the arrest of Sinyavsky and Daniel have been organized in recent years. Sixty-three Moscow writers joined together in petitioning for their release from confinement. News has leaked out of riots and mass disturbances brought on by other causes.

Eugene Lyons provides a vivid description of some recent disturbances in his book *Worker Paradise Lost*:

> Bloody riots are known to have erupted at Temir-Tau in the Karaganda region in 1959; at Novocherkassk in the Rostov area in 1962; at Pskov in 1963. In Tillis, the capital of Soviet Georgia, in March 1956, there were huge demonstrations, in which thousands, mostly young people, fought from behind barricades. The government threw tanks and heavy artillery against them; estimates of the dead ran as high as seven

hundred.

The Novocherkassk tragedy is worth recounting because, after years of rumor and guesswork, the facts were brought out and made public by eye-witnesses who escaped to the West. In June 1962, demonstrations against the government were touched off in a number of areas by the announcement of higher prices for meat and dairy products. Apparently, the bloodiest struggle occurred in Novocherkaask, a city of 100,000 about sixty miles from Rostov.

It began on June 1 as a peaceable student demonstration. Workers left their benches to join them. By the next day, some 20,000 were in the streets. The local militia proved inadequate and uncooperative against the demonstrators. The first regular soldiers brought into the city refused to shoot into the crowds. Moscow then rushed in motorized units of KGB [secret police] troops which did the job of pacification." An eye-witness, writing in *Nashi Dni*, an *emigre* magazine in Germany, said that he counted more than two hundred dead in the central square and that the toll was heavy in other districts.

After the bloodbath, two Kremlin leaders, Mikoyan and Poliansky, flew to Novocherkassk with promises and soothing words. The city was quarantined for six weeks: nobody could leave or enter without a KGB pass. Not a word appeared in the press, of course, of course, but soon the story was being talked about in whispers throuhgout the country. The "Budapest of Russia," some called the city.[12]

Any assemblies of persons described as "spontaneous demonstrations" in the Soviet press are certain to have been staged by the authorities. These assemblies are part of the masquerade of democracy fabricated by the Party to delude outsiders. For example, citizens in democratic countries may from time to time protest actions of foreign governments by demonstrating before their embassies. Why should we not do the same, the Party leaders reason? And so they order a group to demonstrate before the American embassy as an expression of "popular" disapproval of the war in Vietnam. Of course, their demonstrations have nothing in common with those in democratic nations. But who is to know the difference?

Assembly of members of the community for religious worship is objectionable to the Soviet leadership for several reasons, but the leaders have encountered great difficulty in controlling this aspect of life. Atheism is inherent in the Communist doctrine, but a great many Russians are still religious. They are, in the native term, "believers." The Ivanov family will not be prevented from attending church services if they are available, but churchgoers must expect their careers to suffer. In particular, believers, when

---

12 Lyons, E. 1967. *Workers' Paradise Lost*. New York: Funk & Wagnalls, 97.

known, are excluded from the Party and governmental positions.

A church may serve as a place of worship, but it may not propagate the faith except among those training for the clergy. Religious education is, for all practical purposes, forbidden. On the other hand, anybody is free to disseminate antireligious propaganda as a constitutional right, and the school system together with Party organs does so as a regular part of their programs. Some former churches are used by the government as antireligious museums.

It is a fundamental American tenet that church and state must be separated. There is no established religion in the United States, and recent Supreme Court decisions have forbidden religious education and worship of a denominational character in the public schools or other governmental institutions.

A church of any faith may be established and may hold its own property like all other voluntary associations. Contributions to religious institutions are encouraged by allowing them as deductions from taxable income. Church property is not normally taxed. Parents may send their children to parochial instead of public schools if they wish to, and churches themselves are free to engage in religious instruction of any kind.

The family of John and Mary Doe may worship in any faith and manner they choose. They need not worship at all. Their beliefs are strictly their own business. The Constitution explicitly states that "no religious Test shall ever be required as a Qualification to any

Office or public Trust under the United States."

In the Soviet Union, the church is separated from the state but completely dominated by it. No church may own property, including sacramental vestments and vessels. When the Ivanovs go to church, they enter state property and worship at the pleasure of the state. A small parish council is made responsible for the property used by each church. The government, usually under the excuse of bowing to popular demand, may close a church to worship at any time.

Governmental control over churches is now exercised through the State Council for Religious Affairs located in Moscow. For all practical purposes, the council is an arm of the secret police, and its staff is drawn from those ranks. Through regional offices, the council regulates church activities and keeps a close eye on parishioners.

The only clergy authorized to conduct services are those registered with the council. The council also maintains records of members of all congregations, particularly those who are confirmed or married in church. It is therefore relatively easy to prevent known believers from entering Party or government service and to subject them to intensive atheist propaganda.

The largest and most affluent denomination is the Russian Orthodox Church, the established religion of Czarist Russia. His-torically the Orthodox Church was always subordinate to the state, serving as the spiritual support for autocratic rule. Its position is a little different today despite its curious role of providing organized

clerical backing for an avowedly atheist government. Soviet authorities clearly seem to prefer channeling religious activity through
the Orthodox Church, which is accustomed to subjugating itself
to the state.

Rumblings of discontent are being heard, however, from the
clerical ranks of the church, perhaps reflecting deeper unrest among
the faithful. Several courageous theologians and priests have openly
protested subservience of the church to secular authority and pleaded
for a more independent patriarchate. So far the response has been
negative. The protesting priests have been defrocked and the
episcopate warned by the encyclical to observe the dominance of
the state. Such actions merely confirm the facts of power.

Perhaps because they have never been linked so closely with
the state, the Baptists seem to be the most thriving denomination.
Membership now exceeds half a million, having grown fourfold
over the last half-century. Having suffered persecution under both
the Czarist and Soviet regimes, this sect has learned how to stay
within the letter of the law while still offering a haven to the devout.
Its emphasis on religious fundamentals and fervent belief seems to
appeal to the spiritual needs of many Russians today.

The government is particularly hostile toward Roman Catholics,
Jews, and Jehovah's Witnesses. In the last case, the matter is simple.
Since witnesses refuse, as a matter of deep religious faith, to express
allegiance toward symbols of sovereignty, they are disloyal elements

and so must be punished. Soviet rulers are not troubled by the dilemma of conflicting religious beliefs and civil obedience with which our courts so often wrestle. Our Supreme Court has ruled, for example, that schoolchildren may not be required to pledge allegiance to the flag if pledging conflicts with their religious faith. No such compromise is allowed in the Soviet Union. Total obedience to the state comes before all else, and that is that.

In the first two cases, persecution has deep historical roots. The clash with Catholicism is in part the modem continuation of an age-old conflict between Eastern and Western Slavic cultures, the former dominated historically by Russia and the latter by such countries as Poland. The clash has been aggravated by the strong stand taken by the Roman Catholic Church against Communist ideology, in particular, its atheistic orientation.

Anti-Semitism is also embedded in Russian culture. Jews were always treated as lower-class citizens in Czarist days, although they might avoid official persecution by converting to the Russian Orthodox faith. They were often the victims of cruel pogroms, always tolerated and at times encouraged by the government. They were identified as Jews in their passports—which were essential for movement within as well as outside the country—and were thereby denied some of the rights enjoyed by other citizens. With a few exceptions, they were confined to specific regions of the country—the Pale—and were in particular forbidden to reside in

St. Petersburg and Moscow.

Despite vigorous denials, there is ample evidence of discrimination against Jews under the Soviet regime. They still carry passports and identity cards with "Jew" stamped in as their nationality. One of Stalin's last acts was to prepare for a bloody purge based on a fabricated "doctors' plot" against his life, in which Jewish physicians were prominently implicated. It was apparently only his death that stopped the threatened pogrom before it started.

Under Khrushchev, the campaign against "antisocial and parasitic" elements led to widely publicized executions of persons for "economic crimes against the people." Most of those executed had unmistakably Jewish names. The message seemed clear.

Traditional prejudice is not the only source of discrimination against the Jew. Perhaps even more important is the desire of the Communist leadership to eliminate all cohesive communities that might threaten the development of a homogeneous Soviet culture. The problem has loomed larger with the emergence of Israel as a Jewish nation, for the very national allegiance of Russian Jews has become suspect. Now that the Soviet Union has cast itself on the side of the Arabs in their conflict with Israel, internal policy toward the Jews seem to have become an integral part of foreign policy. We must wait to see where this will lead.

Despite persistent controls and constant atheist propaganda over half a century, the Communist Party has not managed to quench the religious spirit of the Russian people. Because so many of them are fervent believers, the Party has had to tread carefully in its program to eradicate religion.

It is true that church services are mainly attended by the middle-aged and the elderly, mostly women. But this may mean only that it is safer for them to make an open display of their faith. Somehow, attendance in the limited number of churches does not seem to suffer from one decade to the next.

No one knows how much less religious the Soviet people are today after a half century of official atheism. It would be strange if the constant antireligious propaganda and absence of religious education had not weakened the religious feelings of at least those who are middle-aged or younger. Whatever faith they have must have been instilled through the family and occasional attendance at church services.

There is no doubt that Communist doctrine takes the place of religion for many Russians. The doctrine can become an object of blind and fervent faith. It has its own rituals and temples of worship, including the mausoleum housing Lenin's body and, at one time, Stalin's as well. During his lifetime, Stalin was worshiped as a god by the faithful.

But the faith of many in Communism has been shaken by the ever-sharpening clash between myth and reality. The denunciation of Stalin by his successors was, in particular, a shock from which those followers who believed he could do no wrong have never fully recovered.

On the part of intellectuals, we witness an unmistakable searching for a new anchor of faith. For some, the answer has come from religion. The religious influence is apparent in the works of Boris Pasternak, author of *Doctor Zhivago*, and of Sinyavsky. Svetlana Alliluyeva, Stalin's daughter, credits her newly found religious faith with crystallizing her determination to defect and ultimately to flee to the West.

It may be that religion will serve as the focal point for the independent thinking so feared by Soviet rulers and so thoroughly controlled elsewhere. This message may be contained in a charming parable attributed, in an article by Peter Grose in *The New York Times*, to Kornei Chukovsky, a writer of beloved children's stories.

Two small children were playing in a Moscow park when one of them, a young lad, suddenly asked his older playmate: "Is there a God?"

"We Communists don't believe so," the older boy replied without hesitation, "but, of course, maybe He does exist anyway."[13]

---

13 Salisbury, H. (ed.) 1967. *The Soviet Union: The Fifty Years*. New York: Funk & Wagnalls, 97.

IV

Consent of the Governed

There is an anecdote about an American tourist who tried to explain democracy to a Russian worker. "Let me tell you," he said, "what it means to live in a democratic society. I come from a very small town in the center of the United States, a thousand miles from our capital city. Suppose I want to see the President. I simply go to the airport and buy a ticket to Washington. Nothing happens. I land in Washington, catch a taxi, and tell the driver to take me to the White House. Nothing happens. I arrive at the White House and tell the guard I want to see the President. I am shown into his office, walk straight up to him, and say: 'President Johnson, you're nuts!' Nothing happens. That's true democracy for you."

The Russian thought for a moment and then said, "Same thing in my country. I live in small village far from Moscow. I go to train station, buy ticket to Moscow. Nothing happens. In Moscow, I catch taxi to Kremlin. Nothing happens. I ask to see Comrade Brezhnev. They take me to him and I say: 'Comrade Secretary, President Johnson is nuts!' Nothing happens. So, we have democracy, too."

Russians are ruled from above and have been for centuries. They know what it means to receive and obey orders. Conditions are more relaxed today, but the memories of Stalin's reign of terror linger along with the scars it caused.

The world does not know the full toll of that terror and perhaps never will, but it runs to millions of lives, not to mention the sufferings of countless others. It was Lenin who introduced the instrument of terror to stamp out opposition to the new regime, and Stalin who developed it to gruesome perfection.

But he pushed too far, straining the incredible endurance of the Russian people to the breaking point. Sensing this and the guilt feelings and moral indignation plaguing the conscience of the managerial class and the intellectuals, his successors have relaxed their grip and searched for less ruthless means of controlling society.

Remember that the founders of the Soviet Union introduced the totalitarian state to the world. It differs from earlier forms of tyranny, such as Czardom, in attempting to control all aspects of social life, not merely the customary relations between subject and sovereign. Everything is made part of the political order, which is itself run by a tight dictatorship.

It was Lenin's genius to recognize the importance of embellishing the Soviet system with the trappings of democracy. If the people want a constitution, give them one, and even include a bill of rights. If they want a parliament, give them that too. And a system of courts. If they want a federal system, create that myth as well. Above all, let them have elections, for the act of voting is what the common man most clearly associates with democracy. Give them all these, but make sure that they have no effect on how things are run.

There are elections in the Soviet Union, but they bear little resemblance to the democratic voting process as we know it. Our government is elected at all levels, from city and county to nation. The basic conditions for elections are specified in the federal and state constitutions. Elections must be held at regular intervals, and in the meantime, any officeholder is subject to removal for misconduct by recall or impeachment and trial. While the specific arrangements will differ from state to state, any qualified voter who meets the age and, in a few cases, other special requirements for office may stand for election if he can muster the support of a moderate number of voters for his candidacy.

Each successively lower level of government in our federal system has an important measure of autonomy over its own affairs. Local governments, for example, have the power to impose their own taxes and to dispose of their own revenues. Actions taken within their spheres of jurisdiction are not subject to reversal by state officials. The same applies to the relations between state and federal governments.

Ours is a government of representatives who can be replaced when they cease to represent their constituents. Public opinion polls keep the officeholders informed on attitudes of the electorate between elections. John Doe will not hesitate to write his congressman or even the President if he has sufficiently strong feelings about an issue, and they pay attention to their mail.

John may visit his representatives when he finds himself in his state or national capital. He will attend meetings of his city or county council and speak his mind. He signs petitions for various causes. All have an impact on how the government is conducted.

In order to keep our government responsive to the popular will and at the same time prevent a complete turnover of government as a result of temporary swings in opinion, terms of office are normally staggered for the various branches of government. At the federal level, we elect our House of Representatives, which is apportioned strictly on the basis of population, every two years. Senators, who represent states of widely differing populations, are elected for six years, but a third of them must stand for election every two years, at the same time that members of the House are chosen. In keeping with our system of separation of powers, the President and Vice

President are elected at yet a different interval, every four years, coinciding with every other congressional election.

There is nothing sacred about this system, which was defined in the original Constitution, and proposals for change are offered now and again for various reasons. Yet it is a tribute to the genius of our Founding Fathers that the system has served so well in providing for responsive government without sacrificing the continuity, stability, and counterbalancing power so essential to the maintenance of a free and flourishing society.

Except for certain local elections, candidates normally run under the banner of a political party, usually the Democratic or Republican Party. In states such as many of those in the South where a single party captures an overwhelming portion of the vote, nominations for office must be made through open primary elections.

No system of representative government can be expected to be perfect or immutable, and many flaws are constantly being found in our own. A society deserves to be called democratic only if there are adequate safeguards for minorities to follow their way of life, express dissent, and agitate for reform. This has not always been so in our country for some racial and ethnic groups, but we take comfort in the fact that the process of government by discussion, taken together with orderly procedures for amending constitutions in response to the popular will, makes possible the gradual elimination of defects.

A democratic system hinges ultimately on open elections by secret ballot. When John Doe enters the polling place, he is ushered into a curtained voting booth. He must mark his ballot or pull the levers of a machine within the privacy of that booth. Nobody is entitled to see how he votes.

Democracy means a great deal more than a simple majority rule in the body politic as a whole. Minorities, which may technically differ from the majority by as little as one per cent, must also be respected and represented. We believe in safeguarding ourselves against the tyranny of the majority as well as the tyranny of a minority. We do so in many ways.

The Constitution provides the most obvious protection of minority interests in its Bill of Rights and other provisions. These spell out the rights of citizens that may not be disturbed by legislative acts, that is, by majority rule. In addition, the Constitution sets forth the principles, processes, and mechanics of our system of government. That set of basic laws is removed from a determination by a simple majority at any point in time. Amendment of the Constitution requires a two-thirds vote of Congress and approval by the legislatures of three-quarters of the states.

We must keep reminding ourselves that no system of government matches exactly the ideal model from which it is cast. The purpose of requiring a highly qualified majority to amend the Constitution is to make sure that no changes are made in our system of government if roughly as much as a quarter to a third of the citizens disapprove of them. The principle of judicial review, on the other hand, may permit the simple majority of the Supreme Court—five out of nine Justices—to amend the Constitution in effect by reversing long-established interpretations of its provisions.

We rely on judicial restraint and various checks over the Court's power in the hands of Congress and the Presidency to minimize the danger of amendment by judicial fiat. But the problem has no easy resolution. It is surely wrong to argue that the Court's decision can, after all, be overruled by an amendment passed through Constitutional procedures, for that would stand the amendment process on its head. Such an argument amounts to saying that the Constitution can be amended if as few as a quarter to a third of the citizens so wish, for that minority can keep the Court's decision from being overruled.

The principle of qualified majorities is also put into effect in the ordinary course of government by providing for representation based on constituencies. For example, the members of Congress might be chosen in a nationwide election, in which case each would, in a contest between two candidates, have to win a majority of all votes cast. Instead, each member is elected in a separate geographical district. Voters may cast their ballots only in the district where they reside, and candidates must reside in the districts in which they run.

How different it is in the Soviet Union. When Ivan goes to the polls, he is handed a ballot listing candidates for various offices. He will note that there is only one candidate listed for each office to be filled. His only choice is to vote for or against the listed candidate. He has no way of voting for somebody else. To vote against a candidate, he scratches the name off the list.

Although he may mark his ballot in the privacy of a curtained booth, he is not required to do so. He knows that many voters make a display of immediately folding their unmarked ballots before the eyes of election officials and placing them in the ballot box. For him to enter a booth is to raise the suspicion that he intends to vote against at least one candidate. With the Party watching over him, he must weigh this decision carefully.

Despite the danger, there are always some scratches but never enough to defeat candidates for the republic or union legislatures. They always receive vastly more votes than scratches. On rare occasions, a candidate for some local body may be defeated.

It will come as no surprise that Soviet majorities are purer than Ivory soap. In the 1962 election for the union legislature, 99.95 percent of eligible voters were reported as casting their ballots. The Party list of candidates was said to have received 99.47 percent of the votes in the case of one house and 99.60 percent in the case of the other. The Soviet press, with characteristic lack of humor, cited these election results as evidence of the absolute solidarity of Party and people.

Perhaps since it hardly matters, candidates do not need to reside in the constituency for which they stand or voters where they vote. A passenger on a train may even vote on election day at any station along the way. To vote, a person must be at least 18 years old and legally sane. The minimum age for candidates is 23 years for the union legislature and 21 years for the republic legislatures.

None of this will seem strange to Ivan, for it has always been so. He knows all too well that his country is really run by the Communist Party. He knows that the constitution is a travesty, particularly when it describes his country as a voluntary union of equal republics, each free to secede at will. Or when it asserts that the Supreme Soviet, a parliament of two houses, is the highest organ of state power with exclusive legislative power.

He must smile when he reads the provisions for resolving a disagreement between the two houses or, in the event of failure, for dissolving parliament and calling new elections. No meaningful debate has ever taken place in either house, and no dissenting vote has ever been cast. The sessions last only a few days and consist of rubber-stamp approval of whatever acts are submitted by the rulers of the country.

The actual governing body is the Council of Ministers and its Presidium. The Chairman of the latter, now Alexei Kosygin, serves as chief executive, but he is subservient to the Secretary-General of the Communist Party. In the latter part of their rule, both Stalin and Khrushchev openly displayed their power by holding both offices. The positions are split at present: Leonid Brezhnev serves as Secretary General. Neither Kosygin nor Brezhnev is technically head of state. That office, largely ceremonial, is filled by the President of the Presidium of the Supreme Soviet, today a gentleman named Nikolai Podgorny.

The Communist Party, the seat of all power, is an organization with only superficial resemblance to political parties in democratic countries. The constitution designates it as "the vanguard of the working people in their struggle to build a communist society" and "the leading core of all organizations of the working people, both public and state." As such, it is the only political organization permitted to exist. Moreover, it is so organized that the division of the membership into viable factions is very difficult to achieve.

In our country, political parties are strictly voluntary associations that may be formed by any group of like-minded citizens who wish to engage in political activity. Each state has laws regulating the organizational plans of parties proposing to field candidates in elections. These regulations are designed to ensure to the rank and file an adequate voice in the selection of party officials and the formulation of policies and platforms.

As anyone familiar with the American political scene knows, each of the two major parties contains a wide spectrum of opinion on political issues, the more critical divergences of viewpoint being represented by rival factions. These differences are nowhere more apparent than at the national conventions held to nominate presidential candidates. The proceedings are viewed by tens of millions of Americans on television, broadcast by radio, and reported in newspapers.

Other political parties abound. Some are active only within the confines of a single state, like the Farmer-Labor Party in Minnesota or the Conservative and Liberal Parties in New York. Others, like the Prohibition Party, are focused on specific issues and become active only in presidential years. Ideology forms the basis for still others, ranging from those consistent with the democratic tradition, like the Socialist Party, to those espousing dictatorship like the Communist and Nazi Parties.

Most Americans feel some party allegiance, and many participate actively in political organizations. They may do so on a continuing basis as regular members or officials, or periodically during election campaigns as volunteers for one set of candidates or another. Our youth in high school or college may engage in partisan activity in various ways through affiliates of political parties. Membership in a host of other nonpartisan organizations concerned with political questions is open to everybody. In short, anybody in the United States may choose among an enormously wide range of activities in the field of politics, covering the spectrum of political beliefs.

In the Soviet Union, on the other hand, the only vehicle for political activity is the Communist Party. It is open only to those who are considered to be absolutely faithful to the ideology and policies of the Party. To become a member, Ivan must apply to the Party unit at his place of work; that is, to those in the Party who are most likely to know him best. He must be recommended by three persons who have been members of the Party for at least three years. If he has belonged to the Communist Youth League, one of those recommendations may come instead from a local committee of that organization.

Those who support an applicant do so at some risk, because they will be held accountable for a mistaken judgment. They may even be expelled from the Party if the applicant turns out to be particularly undesirable.

If Ivan is accepted by the primary group to which he applies and by the next higher unit to which it is subordinated, he becomes a Party candidate for a trial period of a year. He then may be admitted to full membership.

Once admitted, a member does not expect to have much to say about how the Party is run or what its policies are. His duty is to serve in whatever capacity the leadership designates. Like the government and every organization within Soviet society, the Party is organized according to the principle of so-called "democratic centralism," which has nothing at all to do with democracy. It is instead a mechanism for ensuring absolute control from the top within an apparently federated but actually centralized structure.

Full subordination of all lower units is accomplished through two channels: first, a hierarchical bureaucracy that reaches from top to bottom and, second, a system of administrative echelons in which each may overrule all decisions, or intervene in any other way, at lower levels.

The Party structure consists of a pyramid formed from successive tiers of conferences, each composed of delegates selected by the next lower tier, culminating in the All Union Congress of the Communist Party. These conferences do little except to meet infrequently—every other year by current practice—when committees are selected to supervise day-to-day affairs. Each committee, in turn, selects an executive board from its membership to serve as the effective officers of the Party. At the top, corresponding to the All-Union Congress stands the Central Committee with the Politburo of eleven members and nine candidate members as its executive board and a separate permanent Secretariat as its administrative apparatus. Brezhnev heads both the Politburo and the Secretariat.

The purpose of the Communist Party is simple: to preserve control of the country by a small self-perpetuating elite. Members and delegates may express some personal views in meetings, but once a vote is taken—always by a show of hands—every member is absolutely bound to abide by the decision and to implement it without question.

The Party is a well-disciplined army that obeys its commander-in-chief, the Secretary General. The controlling element is the full-time professional apparatus, a party within the Party. Together with the secret police, it forms the foundation of power on which the system rests.

Of course, membership in the Party does no harm to one's career, and we should expect many members to be opportunists with little allegiance to principle or person. To guard against capture of the Party by these and other types of independent thinkers, the apparatus has tried to restrict membership by intellectuals and other highly educated persons. In recent years, however, they have come to account for half or more of all members, a situation that is undermining the power of the apparatus.

In Stalin's day, there was no question who was the boss of the Soviet Union. He held all power in his grasp. Khrushchev had less complete authority, and today the controls are even more diffuse. Nobody outside the select little group in the Politburo knows exactly how final decisions are made, but we can be sure that they are made there.

The actual machinery of government lies outside the Party organization, but there is a parallel Party organ corresponding to every governmental office. Moreover, all governmental officials are Party leaders of comparable rank. Finally, as we come full circle, by maintaining absolute control over the composition of all legislative bodies, the Party prevents the rise of a competing base of power.

The tyranny of the Soviet system is made complete by not allowing the citizens to "vote with their feet." Nobody can choose the nature of the political order into which he is born, but at least he can have the freedom to escape. Not so in the Soviet Union.

First of all, residence and travel within the Soviet Union are controlled by a rigid internal passport system, which we shall consider in more detail at a later point. An urban resident is permitted to move to another locality only if he obtains a job or enters a school there. Those who live in rural areas—about half the population—are denied passports unless they are hired by the state to work in a town or admitted to a school there. A person without a passport is not legally entitled to remain in a town for more than five days at a time. Hence, like the serfs of Czarist times, peasants are effectively tied to the land.

Secondly and more importantly, nobody is allowed to leave the Soviet Union without an external passport, which is granted as a privilege and not a right. To enforce this prohibition of unauthorized departure, troops patrol a strip more than a mile wide on the frontiers encircling this vast country. Entry into this strip is forbidden except as authorized by the frontier guards. An adjoining zone of considerable width is closed to everyone but those registered as residents.

If a Soviet citizen defects once he has been allowed to leave the country, he cannot renounce his citizenship without permission of the state. In the eyes of the Soviet government, citizenship lasts for life regardless of the desires of the individual involved. Any citizenship a defector may acquire elsewhere is not recognized by the Soviet state. If he returns to the Soviet Union, he is subject to punishment as a traitor.

Until recently the law was especially severe in the case of members of the armed forces who fled abroad. The families they left behind were subject to imprisonment for no less than five and up to ten years. Although not explicitly stated in the criminal code, similar treatment might well have been accorded to the families of important personages who defected. It is difficult to imagine any principle more cruel and unjust than the one of the collective responsibility of the family for criminal acts by one of its members.

In the United States, we are blessed with complete freedom of movement for all citizens, both within and outside the country. Every citizen has the right to vote with his feet. Because of our federal system, he may leave one state whose political, economic, or social conditions he does not like and moves to another. The Constitution guarantees this right in stating that "the Citizens of each State shall be entitled to all Privileges and Immunities of Citizens in the several States." Finally, he may leave the United States temporarily or permanently at any time he wishes to. And he may renounce his citizenship at will.

As a matter of practice, passports have come to be necessary for travel to and from most, though not all, areas abroad, but the

Supreme Court has been strict in ruling that no citizen may be denied a passport. The State Department has claimed the right to withhold a passport from a citizen if he explicitly states that he intends to use it in travel for which the passport is declared to be invalid. Normally, such use involves travel to specified countries with which we do not have diplomatic relations. The courts have, however, ruled against the State Department.

We may be thankful to the Court for standing by long-established precedent in safeguarding our precious liberty to leave. Nothing more clearly marks the boundary between the Communist and democratic worlds than the Iron Curtain and the Berlin Wall erected on the Communist side to imprison their people. If we adhere to our democratic tradition, we shall resist with determination any temptation on our part to raise barriers to keep our own citizens at home, whether by means of a "travel tax," a gold wall (efforts to restrain movements and preserve our stock of gold), or any other device. There are no problems—economic, political, or social— that require for their solution a denial of the fundamental liberty to leave. A denial of that liberty would signify a major and perhaps irretraceable step away from democracy.

We may appreciate the blessings of self-government more by reflecting on the plight of Ivan and Anna Ivanov, captives of their oppressive regime. They and their fellow citizens have of necessity learned to submit, for they have no alternative.

Yet there are growing signs of political unrest. Some prominent citizens are calling for a greater voice on the part of the regular membership of the Party. Others cautiously urge that legislative bodies begin to assume some of the authority assigned to them by the constitution. Perhaps Ivan Ivanov himself yearns for some say in the political affairs of his country, but as of now, he is resigned to things as they are. When he hears that a once exalted leader has been suddenly deposed for incompetence, Ivan shrugs his shoulders and goes on with the everyday business of life.

He views politics as squabbling in the ruling household. And what happens in a strange family is none of his affairs.

V

Due Process of Law

When Nikita Khrushchev was recounting Joseph Stalin's crimes before the Twentieth Party Congress in 1956, so the story goes, a voice suddenly called out from the audience: "And where, Nikita Sergeevich, were you when all this was going on?" Khrushchev interrupted his speech, looked out over the audience, and asked, "Will the person who said that please rise?"

A heavy silence hung over the hall. No one stirred from his seat. Khrushchev surveyed the audience slowly and returned his eyes to the manuscript before him. Then, speaking deliberately, he said, "That, my dear comrades, is where I was."

Many Russians recall the days, at the height of Stalin's terror, when they sat fearfully by the door, a packed suitcase at hand, awaiting the knock that would announce imminent death or imprisonment. Starting as a campaign to liquidate the kulaks (peasants who hired any labor) and then spreading as a political purge, these waves of terror rippled across the entire society until they engulfed tens of millions of victims.

Only the top leaders of the Party and the highest officials of the secret police know the full story of this grim era. Although Khrushchev and his successors have denounced Stalinist terror and vowed to prevent its return, they have not yet summoned up the courage to publish the macabre details. If the cold statistics have not been issued, the personal suffering and indignities have been graphically portrayed in such works as Alexander Solzhenitsyn's masterly novel, *A Day in the Life of Ivan Denisovich*, and Eugenia Ginzburg's autobiographical *Journey into the Whirlwind*. Perhaps there is no need for an official history as far as the Russian people are concerned. It seems likely that virtually every family was touched by terror to some degree. Untold thousands were tortured and executed. Millions were imprisoned. One responsible estimate, based on a careful study of all available evidence, places the smallest number of inmates in prison and forced-labor camps at eight million during the 1940s, and the largest number at twenty million.

If these figures are correct, prisons and concentration camps never held less than one adult out of every ten in this period, and at times they held one out of every five. Subjected to beastly conditions, the inmates were fortunate to survive their terms of confinement, and more than a quarter probably did not.

How did this happen? Khrushchev has given the answer that Stalin was a sick man, demented with paranoia. No doubt there is truth in what Khrushchev says, but it cannot serve as an explanation. There remains the question: How did a madman manage to gain and retain despotic control over the country? An important part of the answer lies in the autocratic apparatus of the Soviet state, much of which remains unchanged even though Stalin has left the scene.

Soviet Communism implies, by its very nature, a system of arbitrary government. The will of an elite, determined to perpetuate itself in power, cannot be reduced to a set of impersonal and impartial laws governing relations among subjects. Convinced of their infallibility, the self-chosen rulers see no reason to tolerate disagreement or disobedience. Their aim is to get things done: The end dominates the means. They get things done by issuing orders, now in this direction, now in that. What the rulers do is, after all, for the good of "the people," and anybody who stands in their way is, therefore, an enemy of "the people." He must be removed.

It is a cardinal precept of the Soviet system that a crime against the state—read "the people"—is more vicious than a crime against a fellow human being. A worker who pilfers goods from his factory, an engineer who causes his train to run late, a speculator who buys currencies for resale—all have one thing in common: They have committed crimes against "the people." Under Soviet law at one time or another in recent years, they could be condemned to death —the first and last still can be—while a murderer may merely have to "sit" for a few years, as the slang goes for imprisonment.

Disaffection or, even worse, incitement of disaffection is the gravest crime of all against "the people." The Party leadership feels entirely justified in suspending such legal procedures as there are when it must deal with suspected "wreckers" and "saboteurs."

The Soviet Union maintains a system of courts, but it bears only a superficial resemblance to its counterparts in the free world. The Communist Party selects judges in the same way as it does other governmental officials. Local judges are formally elected by popular vote, but the ballot, as in other cases, contains only one name for each position. All judges serve for limited periods and can be removed and replaced at any time. Virtually all are members of the Party. Prosecutors, who as procurators wield more power than in our country in initiating trials and appeals, are all appointed from the central government by the Prosecutor General of the Soviet Union.

Formally, the procedures in Soviet criminal trials accord with generally accepted standards of justice. The defendant is presumably entitled to be tried in public with oral testimony, to be informed of the charge, to be represented by counsel, to be confronted by witnesses, to introduce evidence, and appeal convictions. In practice, these rights have often been suspended, particularly in cases of alleged crimes against the state. After 1956 many of the specific laws abridging procedural rights were repealed, but one may wonder how meaningful such action was in view of recent trials like that of Sinyavsky and Daniel.

The most glaring shortcoming of the Soviet judicial system, in form as well as substance, is the absence of the presumption that a defendant is innocent until proven guilty. In the period of legal reforms after Stalin's death, some eminent jurists argued strongly for presumption of innocence, but to no avail.

A criminal case is first investigated at a lengthy pretrial hearing at which witnesses are examined and evidence is reviewed. The investigation is conducted by members of the prosecutor's staff in the case of crimes against a person, but always by the secret police in the case of a crime against the state. The defendant, unless he is a juvenile or a mentally incompetent person, is not entitled to counsel during this hearing, which is held before a member of the prosecutor's office. He need not be informed of the charges against him for ten days, and he may be detained for nine months without the right to contact anybody or to seek a writ of habeas corpus. The trial must start within twenty-eight days after nine months of detention, but it may be delayed almost indefinitely thereafter. The findings of the preliminary hearing form the basis of the indictment presented to the court by the prosecutor, and the trial then consists primarily in verification of the facts and findings of the preliminary hearing.

Those sitting in judgment are almost certain to presume the defendant guilty. After all, the prosecutor has reached this conclusion after careful examination of the evidence. Counsel for the defense has, under the circumstances, little to do except challenge the validity of preliminary findings and plead extenuation.

That hardly matters in any event, because all lawyers are members of collective agencies strictly controlled by the state. While the defendant has some latitude in choosing counsel, and a lawyer in accepting or rejecting a case, there is an obvious conflict of interest on the latter's part. The lawyer's career hinges on his remaining in the good graces of the Party, and he is bound to exercise caution in defending an unpopular client no matter what his conscience may dictate. He may be disbarred by the provincial legislature or the Minister of Justice without right of appeal.

There are no trials by jury. Instead, a case is heard by a judge and two lay assessors. The latter are chosen from a panel that has been approved by the Party and hence hardly represents a cross section of the public. Although the lay assessors, along with the judge, enjoy the privilege of participating actively in the trial by questioning and cross-examining witnesses, they have seldom bothered to do so until recently. And their more active intervention has had the effect of injecting more rather than less politics into trials. They are another of the many curious appendages found in Soviet society, borrowed from another culture—in this case Germany—but not employed in the original manner.

Under Soviet law, the severity of a crime is to be judged by its consequences, not by the intent of the perpetrator. The foremost issue is whether an act was "socially harmful." As far as punishment is concerned, it matters little that the act was the result of accident or negligence rather than malice. This concept of crime is indeed foreign to the civilized world, where intent is the crux of the matter.

One might think that it would be difficult to devise a judicial system more heavily weighted against the innocent, but two additional features prevalent in the Soviet past and subject to revival need to be mentioned.

The first is the pernicious concept of "analogy." This principle, not removed from the legal code until 1958, made it possible to convict a person considered to be "socially dangerous" even though he had not broken any law on the books. The judge needed merely to find him guilty of an act somehow similar to one defined as a crime. This principle amounted to nothing more than enactment and enforcement, after the fact, of laws suited to specific individuals. It is difficult enough for a Soviet citizen to know the laws in force, since those that are published are not easily accessible and many are kept secret. It is impossible for him to divine every action that might conceivably be deemed criminal.

It is important to recognize that most laws in the Soviet Union do not emanate, even formally, from the legislature. They are issued in the form of decrees later ratified by the legislature when in session. In addition, there is an enormous volume of administrative regulations with the full force of law that is issuing forth constantly from various agencies of the government. In 1947 one could even witness the comic spectacle of Andrei Vishinsky, then Minister of Justice, appearing before the legislature to suggest that it amend the constitution to conform with existing laws.

In two important respects, crime by analogy still remains in force. First, there are omnibus clauses in many laws that enable virtually any undesirable act to be treated as a crime. For example, there is hardly anything a foreigner might do that could not be called espionage. Second, the laws on socialist property are couched in such sweeping terms that they effectively embrace all activities that might be construed as hampering the interests of the state, that is, as "socially dangerous."

The second feature that needs to be mentioned is the use of the secret police as an independent judicial body. At the beginning of his great purge in 1934, Stalin established special boards in the Ministry of Interior with the power to try and sentence persons suspected of political crimes. These boards were not obligated to follow any normal rules of procedure.

The world is well acquainted with the investigative techniques of Soviet secret police, including every known method of psychological and physical torture. Those techniques have made normally strong-willed men cringe before the courts in which they were tried and abjectly confess the crimes of which they were accused. Perhaps less well known are the millions of cases tried by the special boards in secret, judgment being carried out by summary execution or imprisonment in concentration camps. These special boards were not abolished until Stalin's death, and they could be revived at any moment.

Within the last decade, an institution akin to the special boards, although with more limited power, has in fact been created. The new quasi-judicial bodies are called "social assemblies." They consist in gatherings of workmen, colleagues, or neighbors convened by a committee for public order composed mainly of Party members. Their purpose is to try cases of so-called "antisocial and parasitic" behavior. Upon conviction by a show of hands, the defendant may be sentenced to banishment, but not confinement, in a remote region for up to five years. Recent legislation has confined the jurisdiction of these assemblies, but they form the nucleus for a system of summary political courts whenever it is deemed desirable to reestablish one.

What goes by the name of justice in the Soviet Union, it is clear, has little in common with the rule of law as we know it. The outgrowth of many centuries of democratic development, the rule of law provides for order with freedom and justice. We often summarize our tradition by saying that we seek a government of laws, not men. By this, we mean that some men should not have arbitrary power over the lives of others. We reject the principle of truth and morality by authority.

Laws must be an expression of democratic will, they must be general in nature, and they must apply equally to all, high as well as low. No one, in any position of authority, is above the law. But more importantly, laws may not infringe on the sphere of individual liberty. The rule of law, first and foremost, defines and limits what the government may do, no matter how democratic it may be. It reserves to individuals certain rights in the form of basic freedoms and elemental justice.

It is no accident that the first amendment of our Constitution begins with the words "Congress shall make no law" and continues with an enumeration of some basic freedoms against which no law shall be made. The Constitution then goes on to spell out the rights that every resident shall enjoy in relation to government. These we call our civil rights. It is a fundamental principle of the rule of law that every law must be as explicit and definite as humanly possible. All laws must be published and made accessible to everybody. Except for cases involving juveniles or matters of national security, all trials must be open to the public. Proceedings under the law must be available to all interested parties. There is no such thing as a secret, hidden, or implicit law. An individual may be accused of a crime only if a reasonable and prudent person has cause for believing that he may have broken a definite law in existence at the time.

As we have seen in the Soviet case, it is not enough that these rights be written down on a piece of paper called a constitution. They must be put into effect and preserved by institutions, by practice, and ultimately by strong tradition. All three are interwoven in the American system as it has evolved.

The institutional base rests on the independent legislative, executive, and judicial branches of government, each with separate and counterbalancing powers. Federalism adds a vertical counterpart to this horizontal separation of powers. The purpose is to keep the government as close to the people as possible and to prevent any group within the government from defying the democratic process and usurping power.

Our system rests on dispersion of power, which we view as the only way to preserve a free society. We accept the dictum of Lord Acton, the great English scholar, that "Power corrupts, and absolute power corrupts absolutely." We also know that the corrupt seek power. The more corrupt they are, the more power they seek. Our institutions are designed to prevent concentration of power into the hands of any man or body of men.

To further this end, police powers have been reserved to the states and localities. We have intentionally avoided creating a national police force. The Federal Bureau of Investigation is the closest counterpart, but it is rigidly confined to the enforcement of federal laws and the powers of its agents are deliberately circumscribed.

It is important that these restraints remain effective.

All governmental officials are sworn to support the Constitution. The President takes a special oath to preserve, protect, and defend it. Our courts—ultimately the Supreme Court itself—undertake the special duty of reviewing laws and administrative acts to ensure that they conform with provisions of the Constitution. The purpose of judicial review is not to determine whether laws or acts have had beneficial results, but whether those who enacted or performed them had the authority to do so. Once a democratic framework of government is established, its survival depends on strict observance of the principle of legitimacy.

There are, of course, many gray areas. All laws are supposed to originate in the legislature, yet many administrative orders and judicial decisions take on the character of legislation. Under the "Trading with the Enemy" act passed by Congress during World War I and reactivated in World War II and again later by the declaration of a state of emergency during the Korean War that is still in effect, our President today enjoys the power to rule, in effect, by decree in certain spheres.

Fortunately, these powers have remained largely dormant, but an executive order issued in January 1968 regulating certain property rights of American residents in foreign transactions represents exercise of authority by the Presidency reserved to Congress by the Constitution. This is a case of delegated power that the Supreme

Court may or may not hold to be legitimate if it is challenged. We may hope that this departure from constitutional procedures does not set a dangerous precedent leading to transfer of legislative power to the executive branch. Once again, the lesson is the need for eternal vigilance in preserving a free society.

We have, to use the familiar but apt phrase, a government of checks and balances. We need not delude ourselves that this system of government resolves all problems in the constant search for a proper balance of freedom and order, that it leads always and everywhere to results conforming to some ideal of democracy and justice. Liberty, equality of opportunity, and justice for all remain goals to be striven for.

What we have created is a process whereby social problems, arising from the diversity of individuals and the circumstances in which they find themselves, can be openly discussed and resolved whenever possible through voluntary agreement. The government exists to benefit the individual, to serve him in his quest for fulfillment of his own values, to protect his life, liberty, and property.

Some will argue that our government is not strong or big enough, others that it is too strong and big. Some will praise recent political trends, others will condemn them. We will not concern ourselves with such questions here. For our purpose, it is sufficient to pose the sharp contrast between the Soviet system of authoritarian dictatorship and the American system of democratic rule of law, as they exist here and now.

The contrast is perhaps nowhere more striking than in the treatment of those accused of a crime. In the first instance, a person may be arrested in the United States only if a warrant for his arrest has been issued or if the arresting person has probable cause for believing that an offense is being or has been committed, in his presence in the case of a misdemeanor. Upon arrest and before any questioning proceeds, the accused must be cautioned of his right to have counsel and not to incriminate himself.

He is protected against unreasonable search and seizure of evidence by the requirement that a search warrant normally must be issued. He must be quickly charged with a specific crime and arraigned before a magistrate. Except for capital offenses, the accused is entitled to release on bail. An indictment by grand jury or "information" by comparable authority must be handed down before he can be tried.

The rights of an accused under trial are described with remarkable clarity by the Constitution: "In all criminal prosecutions, the accused shall enjoy the right to a speedy and public trial, by an impartial jury of the State and district wherein the crime shall have been committed, which district shall have been previously ascertained by law, and to be informed of the nature and cause of the accusation; to be confronted with the witnesses against him; to have compulsory process for obtaining witnesses in his favor, and to have the

Assistance of Counsel for his defense." These requirements apply literally to federal courts, but they have been gradually extended to the states through interpretation of the Fourteenth Amendment. Today the right of the accused to subpoena witnesses is the only one still lacking in some states.

In brief, an accused is just that and nothing more. He is presumed innocent until found guilty beyond a reasonable doubt by a jury of his peers. He may not be compelled to testify against himself, and he may not be convicted on his confession alone unless he pleads guilty. Recent decisions of the Supreme Court have even held that a confession, although otherwise valid, is not admissible evidence if the accused has been denied, in ways specified by the Court, due process of law in the proceedings against him. Once found innocent, he may not be tried again for the same offense.

At all stages in a proceeding against him, an accused is entitled to counsel chosen by himself or, in the event of indigence, appointed by the court. He has at his disposal a multitude of lawyers engaged in private practice with no interest in seeing him convicted and an incentive to defend him faithfully. His deliberations with counsel constitute privileged information, inadmissible as evidence in his trial. His counsel is not expected to duplicate judge and jury by carefully and impartially weighing evidence, but instead to plead the strongest possible case for him.

Many judges—all, in federal courts—are appointed for life

subject only to good behavior, in an effort to remove them as far as possible from political influences. They must be trained in the law. Juries are chosen jointly by prosecution and defense from panels that must represent a cross-section of community life.

The contrast between the two legal systems is clear. Ours is designed to protect the innocent individual against the threat of the state. The Soviet system is designed to protect the state against the threat, potential as well as actual, of the individual. The one system is based on pluralistic individualism, the other on authoritarian collectivism. It may be, as many argue, that we have gone too far in safeguarding the accused at the expense of public order, thereby contributing to the growing problem of crime. But any reasonable redress of the balance would still leave the two systems poles apart.

At the moment, terror has subsided in the Soviet Union as an instrument of power, but its ingredients remain imbedded in the political order. To eradicate actual and incipient resistance to authority, the Soviet state naturally and intentionally employs capricious and unpredictable punishments. Better that the citizen does not know the law. Let him beware of the state. Let him obey absolutely, doing what he is told and not what he believes he can get away with.

A return of Stalinist terror is probably not in the offing, but neither is any leap toward liberalization.

VI

An Informed Citizenry

A democratic society rests on an informed citizenry, mindful of important issues and facts and ever critical in its searching for the truth. Diverse sources of information must be available and subject to constant examination and evaluation in the public forum. The electorate must be sufficiently well-educated to engage in this deliberative process and for governing itself effectively and wisely.

In the United States, we have developed an environment of traditions and institutions favoring these ends. While providing a basic education for all, we cultivate a spirit of free inquiry and expression and safeguard their practice. Free speech and a free press serve as the vehicles of open discussion, in which competing and conflicting ideas and facts are subjected to the test of critical analysis.

In no other nation of the world at any time has the government been put to so much work in gathering, processing, and disseminating information for the benefit of the public. It was fortunate that our Constitution called from the beginning for a census of the population every ten years so that our House of Representatives could be reapportioned periodically on the basis of an accurate count of the people it serves. Over the years the scope of the census has been vastly expanded, and a great many other fact-gathering activities have been undertaken at all levels of government. This enormous fund of information, far from perfect but more complete than that available to any other people, serves us all: our representatives in their tasks of running the government, the various social and economic groups in the pursuit of their interests, the common man in the ordinary business of life, and the scholar in his studies.

But we recognize that it would be fatal to grant government anything approaching a monopoly over the supply of information. No group in power, even though motivated by the best of intentions, can be expected to resist the temptation to mobilize facts for its own purposes. The line between information and propaganda becomes thin to the vanishing point when there are no checks on the pronouncements of government.

One such check is built into our political system in the form of federalism, representative government, separate and counterbalancing powers, and the two-party system. Those who are in power today may be out tomorrow, and they must keep this in mind. No sanctity attaches to official data of the past or present, for they are subject to constant challenge by both ins and outs and are constantly subjected to it. Since the ins will be partisan in their use of facts, it is fortunate that the outs will also be. In this way the general public has an opportunity to weigh the pros and cons in seeking the truth, and it may be aided in doing so by various disinterested scholars.

Even more important checks are provided by the diversity of private sources of information supplemented by an inquisitive and critical press. Many private organizations collect and disseminate information. True enough, many have axes of their own to grind, but this is not an unmixed fault, for the pursuit of a special interest often leads one to seek out and challenge statements by others that might otherwise be uncritically accepted. We might hope that more qualified individuals, particularly among those who dedicate their careers to scholarship, would seek the truth for its own sake and speak out accordingly. Lacking that, we may be grateful for a multitude of special pleading.

It would be wrong to say that John Doe hears with equal intensity all the voices trying to speak to him. The administration in power has greater access to news media than the opposition. Data from official sources are likely to be given greater prominence than those from private ones. In brief, John Doe will surely be subjected to some propagandizing by his government, but he has nonetheless a real opportunity to find other sources of information. They exist, and they have their spokesmen in both the popular press and elsewhere.

Ivan Ivanov is not so fortunate. Unless he engages in the dangerous practice of listening to foreign broadcasts, reading foreign literature, or talking to foreign visitors, he has only one source of "the facts": the Soviet state. No one else in the Soviet Union is entitled, under threat of severe penalty, to collect or publish information of any kind. We have already noted how ruthless the government is punishing those who attempt to do so or who take it upon themselves to discuss official pronouncements in a critical manner.

This is no wonder since the object is to create an obedient citizenry, not an informed electorate. The purpose of information in the Soviet Union is to indoctrinate and propagandize, to instill attitudes in the populace that will ensure political conformity, and to induce behavior that will further the power of the ruling elite.

The Communist Party has no difficulty in rationalizing this thought control. It has, after all, mastered the "science of history" through the writings of Marx and Lenin as interpreted by the current priesthood. There is no need for further inquiry. All that is necessary is to guide the inevitable and therefore—in the curiously inverted morality of Communism—desirable course of history. Of course, the real point is to preserve autocratic power.

In this strange Communist world, anything is "true" if it serves a political end. Nothing is objectively true except the class-struggle theory of history. Facts have no importance in and of themselves unless they serve the task of "building Communism." Hence Ivan is told only what his leaders believe will make him think and behave in the proper way, whether it is true or not.

As a result, facts are distorted and suppressed at will. Scarcely any official data, the only information available, can be taken by Ivan or an outsider at face value. One must always ask: What are they trying to prove? In addition, there is a perpetual air of mystery and secrecy overhanging all events, even the most common. Who needs to know? Information is propaganda, and propaganda is a political instrument.

The Soviet Union is, in a word, a closed society, and the Iron Curtain a reality as much inside the country as out. Foreign correspondents have even been informed recently that it is a crime for them to contact private citizens for any purpose without prior governmental approval. The strict controls make it impossible for an observer to know for sure what is going on in any sphere of life. Some critical knowledge, some relevant facts, some commonplace statistics are always missing. Study of the Soviet society is an exercise in archaeology, in which the patient analyst tries to assemble a gigantic jigsaw puzzle with more than half the pieces missing, just as the archaeologist imagines a vase from a few shards.

The object of Soviet rulers is, of course, to fashion an image that will help to keep them in power. And so it is with formal education as well.

A local Party boss once paid a surprise visit to a class in an elementary school, so the story runs, and asked the teacher who was the brightest pupil. "Sasha, without doubt, comrade," she replied. "He is five years ahead of the class."

"Very well, Sasha, tell me: Who are the three greatest enemies of the Soviet people?"

Sasha rose and responded smartly, "First, there is Comrade Stalin."

"Very good. And second?"

"Comrade Khrushchev."

"Excellent, excellent! Now, third?"

Sasha thought for a moment and then said, "Comrade Brezhnev."

"You are absolutely right!" the Party man exclaimed to the teacher. "This young man is indeed five years ahead of his class!"

An equally important function of elementary education is to prepare the masses for a host of tasks of an unskilled and semiskilled nature and to lay the groundwork for further training of those who will be selected to enter skilled occupations and professions. The educational system is designed to fill quotas for various types of labor set in advance by the central planning authorities. The planned quotas come first. The structure of the school system and the nature of training programs are set in accord with them. In this respect, the Soviet educational establishment functions like a military organization. The concept of knowledge for its own sake or for cultural enrichment is essentially foreign to it.

In the United States, by contrast, education is viewed in an entirely different light. One important objective is to provide all citizens with a basic fund of knowledge and analytical skills that will enable them to participate intelligently in the process of governing themselves. To that end, we attempt to ensure universal education by requiring attendance at approved schools through the midteens.

While creation of an informed electorate is important, it is only one of several purposes of education as conceived in the American tradition. Knowledge may be substituted within limits for deficient endowments of other kinds to help the less fortunate improve their station in life. In a perfectly just world, everybody would perhaps be allowed to choose his parents. Failing that utopia, we can at least open educational opportunities to those who would overcome obstacles placed before them by circumstance. More than this, we believe that the individual should be free to learn in order to pursue happiness as he sees it, and the truth for its own sake. Knowledge is, in our view, the real frontier of progress, a frontier to be explored by each in his own way.

Until recent years, there was little place in our thinking for the notion that education should serve as a means for training citizens to serve the nation in predetermined ways. Our attitude seems, however, to be rapidly changing, and we witness a swelling tide of programs, usually administered at the federal level, directed toward specific "national objectives." The changing emphasis is clearly revealed in the title of one of the more ambitious pieces of legislation of this type, the National Defense Education Act. A great variety of other federally sponsored programs are springing up, each aimed at channeling research toward a planned goal or at training persons for jobs considered desirable by some bureaucratic entity.

There can be no doubt that the character of American education, particularly at the higher levels, is being altered by this trend, and perhaps we should pause and ponder where the path is leading. It will do us no harm to remind ourselves constantly that our heritage calls for education to serve the individual in whatever way he, and not somebody else, chooses.

Whatever may be the trend, the contrast between Soviet and American concepts of education remains sharp. In this country, the primary objective is to help the individual to fulfill his own goals in life, while in the Soviet Union it is to marshal the citizenry into service of the state's goals.

How is Ivan educated? First of all, he attends a school that is run by the central government, even though it is technically administered in the so-called republic in which he resides. In this formal respect, we should recognize that the Soviet system, although strange to us, does not differ from many of those in continental Europe and other parts of the world. Enrollment, curriculum, and examinations are all prescribed by the national government.

Attendance is now compulsory through the first eight years of elementary school, which are divided into two equal segments of four years each. Such statistics as are available indicate that about 98 percent of those in the school-age population currently complete this elementary schooling, but there are reasons to believe that the true percentage is lower. The quality of instruction varies widely from one locality to another, being best for upper-income districts in the largest cities and worst for remote rural areas.

If Ivan is somewhere within the top quarter to three-quarters of his class, depending on whether he lives in the countryside or the city, he may continue into a secondary school. For the country as a whole, something more than half of the graduates of elementary schools are admitted to either a general or special secondary school. In both cases, schooling lasts for two additional years.

The general secondary school has the dual purpose of serving as terminal education for those who are considered qualified to enter the more highly skilled occupations and as preparatory education for the select group destined to enter institutions of higher learning. The special secondary schools, on the other hand, are oriented strictly toward vocational training. In addition to these regular schools, part-time and correspondence courses are offered to those who have jobs, but the quality of instruction is notoriously poor. Many workers are enrolled in these courses, but relatively few receive diplomas.

Pupils attend regular schools six days a week, and their studies consume long hours outside the classroom. The regimen is so severe that some Soviet educators have expressed concern over its adverse effect on the health of the young. The trend is toward lightening the burden of studies.

The American school system is different in many important respects. First of all, it is administered at the local level in the form of both public and private schools. Each state sets its own educational standards, and in conformity with them local school boards, normally elected, erect public schools, operate them, and determine the curriculum. More than nine-tenths of the funds needed to finance public schools are raised from local and state sources.

As a constitutional right, parents may send their children to qualified private schools, parochial or nondenominational, if they wish to. Private schools account today for more than an eighth of total school enrollment, and their share is rising. In a few states, there is a voucher system whereby John Doe may receive a refund of the cost of sending his child to a public school if he sends him instead to a private one.

Local control and the mixed system of private and public schools are deeply ingrained in the American tradition for several good reasons. Foremost is the well-grounded fear that centralized direction of education could lead to abuse of power over the minds of the young. Arguments can of course be made that schooling might be improved in some localities by subjecting them to control from afar, but by the same reasoning it would be worsened elsewhere. Educators are no less fallible than other mortals, and no small elite chosen from among them by a distant government is likely to know the best way of educating children drawn from a great variety of circumstances. While the wise decisions of a national school board would be spread throughout the land, so would the mistakes. For all these reasons, we prefer to rely, as in other areas, on diversity, experimentation, and competition as the engines of progress in the field of education.

Attendance at school is generally compulsory through the age of sixteen, and almost three-quarters of American youth today graduate from high school. More than half the graduates go on to college. The others have many opportunities for further vocational training in various public and private schools and on the job. They may study a great variety of subjects inexpensively through extension, parttime, and correspondence courses.

The American student is usually subjected to a less rigorous discipline than his Soviet counterpart. He normally goes to school five days a week, and homework takes up less of his time outside the classroom. The more leisurely pace of study in and out of the classroom is offset by more years in school, less learning by rote, more reliance on individual initiative, and more emphasis on extra-curricular activities. It is not correct to say that the Soviet pupil is more intensively educated unless one is willing to grant that the content of Soviet education is preferable to ours.

Because of the nature of Soviet society and the purpose of its schools, the curriculum is heavily weighted toward mathematics, science, and technical subjects. The humanities and social sciences have no place for their own sake. They are taught only as a means of indoctrinating the youth with Communist ideology. On the other hand, those with the requisite talents have access to excellent schools for the fine and performing arts.

In the Soviet Union, all textbooks are centrally selected. An elementary history textbook says the following: "Life is difficult for the working classes in all capitalist countries. In the USA, for example, there are about five million unemployed. They are strong, healthy persons, wishing to work but unable to find it. The capitalists are the masters in capitalist countries. Plants, factories, and railroads belong to them."

A secondary geography textbook states: "The United States has many secondary and higher schools and well-equipped hospitals. However, the greater part of the working masses cannot get an education; and a long illness, requiring medical care, also infringes on the material welfare of the well-to-do professional workers. The cost of education and medical care is too great for the majority of

Americans. Also expensive are living quarters in the well-built houses. Therefore, low-paid workers often huddle in old homes."

A secondary history textbook asserts: "After the war, the foreign policy of the USA acquired an extremely aggressive character. The American imperialists openly made known their pretensions for world supremacy. They began the 'cold war' against the socialist countries."

These quotations are typical of countless others that are fed to Soviet youth in the name of education.[14]

In the United States, the curriculum of elementary and secondary schools is much more varied, less specialized, and less doctrinaire than in the Soviet Union. We have no grounds for believing that our system cannot be improved, and it is easy to point out faults and weaknesses that could be eliminated. Yet our basic orientation remains sound.

We want to develop self-reliant citizens who can live their own lives and govern themselves. For these reasons, we have emphasized the liberal arts along with the basic skills of reading, writing, and counting. Perhaps we have underemphasized mathematics and the hard sciences, but we may correct this mistake without taking the Soviet system of education as our model.

---

14 Soviet textbooks cited by Seymour M. Rosen in U.S. Congress. 1966. *New Directions in the Soviet Economy*. Joint Economic Committee. Washington Printing Office, III, 832-833.

Higher education in the two countries differs in essentially the same respects. About 40 percent of the graduates of institutions of higher learning are engineers in the Soviet Union as compared with about 10 percent in the United States. In economics, law, and related fields, the respective percentages are 9 and 17; in educational and cultural fields, 36 and 65; in health, 8 and 6; and in agriculture, 9 and 2. The relatively heavier orientation of the Soviet system toward training individuals for planned tasks in the economy is apparent.

All institutions of higher learning in the Soviet Union are run by the state. In the United States, on the other hand, half the institutions are privately operated, and they account for a third of the students.

Since 1956, no tuition is charged for Soviet higher education, and about four-fifths of the students seem to receive stipends, quite small by our standards, that vary according to need and scholarly performance. The cost of a college education in our country varies so greatly among private and public institutions and from one state to another that it is impossible to generalize. However, few able students are denied a college education for lack of funds, as we can recognize when we raise the question of how many citizens actually achieve various levels of education. On this score, no other country matches ours.

If we accept Soviet statistics at face value, even though they are suspect, about the same fraction—98 percent—of the young now complete the eighth grade as in the United States. At this point, however, the figures diverge sharply. About 93 percent complete the tenth grade here as compared with only 30 percent there. Around 72 percent of American youth graduate from high school or twelfth grade and 40 percent enter college. In the Soviet case, only 12 percent of the relevant age group are admitted to institutions of higher learning, which we must remember start their programs with the eleventh grade. Finally, about 20 percent of our youth complete four years of higher education as compared with only 8 percent of theirs.

In other words, John Doe has at least three times as large a chance of completing 10 years of schooling as Ivan Ivanov, seven times as large a chance of completing 12 years, and four times as large a chance of completing 14 years. It should be recognized, however, that no other country in the world comes as close to the United States as the Soviet Union in providing education for the masses if we leave aside the question of its content.

Another way of assessing the educational attainment of a country is to array the adult population from those with least to those with most education and to mark off the number of years of schooling exceeded by the upper half. This figure is called the median years of schooling, and it is now 6.5 for the Soviet Union and 11.9 for the United States. These figures reflect, of course, past as well as present educational effort, and they will rise in the future, more so for the Soviet Union than for the United States, in response to an upward trend in effort in both countries. Projections suggest that by 1985 the median years of schooling will reach 8 for the Soviet Union and 13 for the United States.

We have long been aware of the fact that educational opportunities vary widely in our country among regions, economic classes, and racial and ethnic groups. Many of our recent programs have been aimed at correcting these inequities, and there is general agreement that much remains to be done despite widespread disagreement on the best ways to do it.

While acknowledging such shortcomings here, we should not suppose that they are in any sense absent in the Soviet Union. Quite the contrary. Ivan's opportunities depend much more on the accidental circumstances of birth than in this country. First of all, as in all other aspects of life, a city dweller has a far better chance than a peasant of moving up the educational ladder. The same is true for those who come from professional or skilled-worker families rather than lower-class ones. There has always been a system of quotas regulating the share of each "nationality" in the student body of institutions of higher learning.

Is Ivan Ivanov better educated than John Doe? The answer must be no. The content and availability of education in the Soviet Union are entirely alien to our way of life. Whatever may be the deficiencies of our educational system, and they are many, it is still dedicated to the individual and not to the state. Improve it we should, but not on the Russian model.

At the same time, we should give due credit to the impressive educational effort of the Soviet Union. Moreover, we may safely assume that, whatever its purposes, the training of minds to think will ultimately react to some degree against the authoritarian state. Though conformity is sought, discontent may be found.

VII

The Pursuit of Happiness

What is the difference between capitalism and Communism?" a Soviet Party boss was supposedly once asked. "As you well know," he quickly replied, "capitalism is the exploitation of man by man. Well, Communism is the precise opposite."

This touch of irony is, of course, not acknowledged in the grim Marxian view of the world. In the eyes of the Communist priesthood, capitalism means simply and plainly the exploitation of downtrodden masses who own no property by the privileged few who do. History is envisaged as a series of class struggles that grow out of the modes of production in the different stages of social evolution. In each stage, one class dominates and exploits another, and the state is nothing more than the instrument of the dominating class. The inevitable course of history discovered once and for all by Karl Marx is said to be a progression from one stage to another as the exploited overthrow their exploiters. Capitalism is the last system before the enslaved propertyless masses - the proletariat - revolt, seize control, eliminate the material basis for warring classes, and create Communism. In this classless utopia, exploitation is by definition to vanish, the state to wither away, and everybody to live together harmoniously without coercion.

Such a view of power relations within a society, while perhaps containing a tiny grain of truth, is fundamentally wrong, as the Soviet Union itself amply demonstrates. And so is the Marxian theory of history, which Communists proudly proclaim as scientific.

There is no grand design in history, no predetermined course. Nor is history a mere jumble of accidents. Chance and choice are its ingredients, together with no small amount of sheer momentum. History is made up of opportunities and constraints, and neither flow mechanically from the nature of man, conscious actions, ideology, customs, institutions, or any other easily identified source. History is instead the product of all these interacting forces, mutually influencing each other.

Our system has grown out of this complex historical process, and it cannot be adequately summarized in a single word like "capitalism." We have already described many of its characteristics, and we may turn now to consider its primary reason for being: the pursuit of happiness by individuals.

The traditional American way of life rests on the twin foundations of freedom of choice and equality of opportunity, never fully achieved but always striven for in greater perfection. We believe that John Doe, given his natural endowments and the objective social conditions surrounding him, should decide for himself how to make his way through life. As long as he is mature and normally competent to make decisions, he is the best judge of his own welfare, and he may do as he pleases, provided that he does not injure others or ignore his familial responsibilities. In brief, each individual claims the right to make his own choices, and by the same token, he must stand ready to accept responsibility for their results. If there are mistakes, let each person make them for himself.

Choice cannot, of course, extend beyond the range of open opportunities. There is no such thing as ideal weather; there is only the best available. And so John Doe cannot control where he was born, but, subject to his material means, he may move to any other place in the United States or to any other country that will accept him. As a child, he must depend on the wisdom of his parents for many vital decisions shaping his life, while the government stands by to protect him against parental abuse. Once on his own, however, he has no one to blame but himself for mistaken judgments.

John Doe is free to choose his own trade and job and to shift from one to another as he wishes. If he is willing to bear the consequences and imposes no harm on others dependent on him, he may devote his life to loafing in one degree or another. Only the society that tolerates the hobo is truly free.

As a worker, John may belong to a union, as about one out of every five workers does. To enter some occupations or to work for some firms, he has no option under existing legislation but to join a union, although some nineteen states now have laws protecting the right not to join. Through unions and similar organizations, workers are permitted to bargain collectively with their employers on wages and other conditions of work, to set up grievance procedures to protect themselves against arbitrary and capricious behavior by their bosses, and ultimately to strike. These rights of organized labor are all subject to restriction in order to limit damage to other affected parties and the general public, and we are constantly trying to achieve the proper balance between the rights of individuals and those of voluntary associations, here as elsewhere.

Just as John Doe may decide how to divide his time between leisure and work, so also may he choose how to dispose of most fruits of his labor. After paying his taxes, by no means an insignificant sum these days, he may divide his income and accumulated wealth as he sees fit among consumption, saving, and investment. As he spends his dollars, he casts his votes in the marketplace, where they wield their proportionate influence over the kinds of activities undertaken by the economy. In response to these relative demands, resources are allocated among literally millions of users through the basic mechanism of competitive enterprise operating within a regime of private property.

Within the gigantic market organized by free enterprise, which still dominates our economy, the consumer is sovereign. The intense forces of competition that continue to rule over at least four-fifths of market activity ensure that the consumer is confronted, when he makes decisions on how to spend his income, with prices that reflect costs of production. Hence, when he spends five dollars on a shirt, he can be reasonably certain that he could not get better value for that amount of money by spending the same sum on something else. By and large, each price represents the value of other things he must give up in order to purchase the item in question. Once he has adjusted his purchases so that each thing is worth to him what he must pay to get it, he can be reasonably sure that there is no way by which he can be provided with more material comforts out of the resources available to him.

In the face of the growing role played by the government in our society, it would be foolish to suggest that each individual is free to shape his own life as this picture may suggest. More than a third of the total net product of our country now passes through the hands of government at all levels, as compared with less than a sixth a generation ago. There are many reasons why this development has taken place, and we cannot survey all of them here, or pass judgment on the accompanying effects. But we may note a few areas in which freedom of choice has been curtailed.

For one thing, laws prescribe the lowest wage for which one may work, a minimum that currently exceeds the average wage in such countries as England. Those who seek jobs but are not sufficiently productive to command that wage are effectively banned from gainful employment. Maximum hours of work at regular rates of pay are also set by law. Many farmers are, for all practical purposes, told what they may produce and how much.

Almost all Americans are required to purchase old-age insurance, and they must do so through the social security program of the federal government; they are not allowed to substitute equivalent private insurance even though it may be cheaper. American businesses and financial institutions are, by virtue of a simple executive order issued by the President, forbidden to enter into certain types of financial transactions in foreign countries, and there have been proposals to impose similar restrictions on the travel of Americans abroad. No individual or private concern is allowed to run a postal service or to engage in a host of other activities reserved for legally protected monopolies, governmental and private. The list could easily be extended, but these few examples are sufficient here.

One important impetus to growth in government has been the desire to improve opportunities for all Americans, though there is considerable disagreement over whether this goal has been best served by the specific programs that have been enacted. Together with freedom and justice, equality of opportunity is one of the basic pillars of the democratic creed. Yet it is not easy to give a precise definition of what it means.

In one sense, it means that people with equal endowments should all have the chance to make the same use of them in the pursuit of happiness. There should be no privilege accorded to one person or burden placed on another because of such irrelevant considerations as ethnic customs, religious beliefs, the color of eyes or skin, and so on. In other words, a person should not be discriminated against for trivial and inconsequent reasons.

In a quite different sense, to make opportunities more equal means to redistribute resources from the more fortunate to the less fortunate. Luck plays a major role in how well one is endowed with those qualities valued by his society: brains, cunning, beauty, at times ugliness, material wealth - in sum, anything rare relative to the demand for it. Some inequities of endowment can be overcome by effort, but others cannot. Some may be countervailed by education, and some by redistribution of income and wealth. But a world of absolute equals is, of course, a will-o'-the-wisp.

We have surely not been as vigorous as we should have been in combating unfair discrimination in American society. Everyone who believes in a civilized and humane society must condemn the coercive segregation of Negroes enforced by law over so many years in various parts of the United States. Fortunately, these barriers are being rapidly removed. We should continue to deplore unfair discrimination in private affairs and attempt to reduce it through persuasion while recognizing that it will weaken only with the passage of time.

In the matter of ameliorating inequalities, our record has been better. Educational opportunities, though always subject to improvement, are open to a far larger part of the population than anywhere else in the world. Income is redistributed through taxation and subsidy. While some obviously live more comfortably than others, there is no strict class system, and there are no class privileges as such. Every man, rich or poor, must wait his turn in line.

The Soviet way of life is so different from ours that it is almost impossible for us to comprehend it. Central planning and privilege stand in the place of freedom of choice and equality of opportunity. As we have noted, the individual serves the state instead of the reverse, and the state consists of the ruling elite.

In the first place, where may Ivan live? This depends largely on where he was born, in the countryside or in the city. The residence is controlled by a domestic passport system, and regular passports, valid for five years at a time, are issued only to those who live in the cities, certain other urban areas, the frontier zone, and the regions neighboring Moscow, Leningrad, and Kiev. No inhabitant of the rest of the country, mainly rural, may have a passport. If he is recruited to work in an enterprise by the special governmental agency for this purpose, he will be issued a temporary passport. The work contract runs for one year at a time on a renewable basis and a temporary passport for three months.

Persons without passports are not legally permitted to visit an urban area for more than five days at a time. This exception is necessary to permit peasants to carry on the ordinary business of life: to bring their meager produce to the collective farm market for sale to the public, to shop for important items not available in the village, and to attend to affairs with various branches of government located only in urban areas. A member of a collective farm may not even move from one farm to another without permission of the management, and then only by reason of marriage or partic-ipation in an official program to settle remote areas. He may leave the collective farm altogether only if officially recruited for labor elsewhere or admitted to a secondary school. In a word, the peasantry, or almost half of the Soviet population, is tied to the land just as it was in the days of serfdom.

The passport is much more than a document of identity, for it contains a historical record of such matters as marital status, employment, residence both permanent and temporary and so on. With the exception already noted for peasants, the law requires that every person who moves about within the passport region must register with the local militia within twenty-four hours after he arrives in a locality and once again when he leaves. He is legally entitled to lodging only if the registration has been entered in his passport.

Every able-bodied citizen of working age, whether he has a passport or not, is issued a workbook identifying him and containing a complete record of education and training, job history with reasons for all separations, and special commendations or rewards. The workbook must be turned over to the employer for as long as a job is held. In the case of certain sensitive jobs, the passport must be surrendered as well, and a special identity card is issued in its place.

The Soviet constitution states that "work is the duty of every able-bodied citizen, according to the principle: 'He who does not work, neither shall he eat.'" That is to say, Ivan is obliged to work whether he wishes to or not. This obligation is enforced in several ways. For example, no one of working age is entitled to housing unless he is currently employed. Those who have no visible legal means of support are considered to be "parasites" and "antisocial elements," and they may be tried by social assemblies and sentenced to banishment in remote areas, as we have already mentioned. In practice, the obligation to work begins at the age of sixteen for all urban residents except students and the handicapped. In the countryside, those who reach the age of twelve must begin working at least fifty days a year.

Between 1940 and 1956 no one could leave his current

employment to take another job without explicit permission from his employer, duly entered into the workbook. Since 1956, workers have been allowed to quit a job on two weeks' notice, but not collective farmers.

Up to about the same time, those young people who did not continue their studies into higher education could be drafted into the labor-reserve program, in which they were trained in various skills for a short period of time and then assigned jobs. The total length of service was four years. This program is no longer in force, and compulsory assignment to jobs applies now only to graduates of special secondary schools and institutions of higher learning for an initial period of three years.

How they are assigned is suggested by a little story about graduation time at a leading technical institute. The graduates were lined up in accord with their rank in the class, and each in his turn was called into an office in which a government official announced the job assignment.

As the first young man entered, he was greeted with the words: "Comrade, I am pleased to inform you that, in view of your splendid academic record, you have been assigned to the finest research institute in Moscow. Congratulations!"

The top graduate drew himself up proudly and responded: "Glory be to you, faithful Comrade, to our beloved leader, Comrade Leonid Ilich Brezhnev, to the all-wise Communist Party, and to the mighty

Soviet Union!"

And so it went down the list until the bottom student was reached.

"Comrade," the official solemnly announced, "it is my duty to tell you that, in view of your record, you have been assigned as an engineer in a gold mine in Eastern Siberia."

The young man sighed and replied: "Glory be to you, faithful Comrade, to our beloved leader, Comrade Leonid Ilich Brezhnev, to the all-wise Communist Party, to the mighty Soviet Union, and to the United States of America!"

"Comrade," the startled official exclaimed, "just what do you mean by that?" "Well," replied the student quietly, "thank God she bought Alaska."

Outside of agriculture, each worker is automatically enrolled in the official trade union designated for his place of work. The primary role of the union is to aid management in enforcing discipline and in making workers exert greater effort to fulfill planned norms. There is no bargaining on wages or conditions of work, and strikes are absolutely forbidden.

Mobility is restrained not only horizontally but also vertically, for Soviet society is highly stratified. To paraphrase George Orwell, all citizens are equal, but some are more equal than others. Movement up the class ladder and its associated privileges are very difficult to achieve. It is much harder to get ahead, to rise above the station of life one is born into, than in the United States.

On the bottom rung stand the peasants, just below the working masses. Next, come the skilled workers and technicians, followed by the professionals and bureaucrats. At the very top are the leading party and government officials. These classes are separated by sharp income differentials, and the disparities among salaries and wages are greater than here. A form of sales tax - averaging about half the retail price of consumer goods - is the principal source of governmental revenue, weighing proportionally more heavily on the poor than on the well-to-do and thereby increasing the inequality of incomes.

A vast array of special privileges is given to the upper levels of social status. Those at the top are accorded the best of everything: spacious housing, country villas, private automobiles, special stores to shop in, first choice of seats at the opera and ballet, and so on. They never stand in line. In a society as drab and thoroughly controlled as the Soviet Union, such privileges make an enormous difference, and they attach in lesser degrees to all the higher levels of the social scale. Ivan Ivanov, our ordinary Russian, knows that he will move into an entirely different world if he can escape from the peasantry into the urban working class, or from the unskilled into the skilled labor category. But everything seems to be against him, from the dead weight of the established social structure to the discriminatory system of education.

As the Ivanovs contemplate their meager earnings from hard

work, they know that virtually all must go for day-to-day living expenses. Except for the upper classes, money in the Soviet Union is meant to be spent. And even when savings are possible, they must take the form of accumulated personal property. Investment in business ventures or income-yielding property is forbidden. Funds may be deposited in savings accounts paying a low rate of interest, and some purchases of durable goods may be made on credit terms.

All payments must be in cash since there are no checking accounts for private citizens in the Soviet Union. If Ivan and Anna save by putting money in a sock, they run the risk of having their hoarded funds eaten away by inflation or confiscated by periodic monetary reforms. In any event, their earnings are normally too low to think about building up a nest egg of any kind.

The Ivanovs are free to spend their income on whatever commodities are available for purchase, but their expenditures will have little influence on what is produced. There is no consumer sovereignty in the Soviet Union. The government determines what goods are to be produced and in what quantities. The so-called collective farm markets, where food grown on both collective farms and private plots are sold at prices set by supply and demand, form the most direct link between consumer and producer. But even here government can control supply by varying the quantities of produce that it procures through its own channels and by changing the volume of resources devoted to agriculture.

Except for these markets, all legal trade takes place through the authorized state network, and prices are set by the state with the dual objectives of absorbing the money income of the population and bringing supply and demand into balance in particular markets. The latter objective is frequently not met, as anyone may see from the queues before some shops and the large stocks of unsold goods that often pile up in others.

There are, of course, many black and gray markets permeating the Soviet economy, for such a rigidly controlled system could not function without them. In principle, all private trading—viewed officially as "speculation"—is a serious crime, but much of it is tolerated nonetheless. Campaigns are launched periodically to eradicate "speculation" of one sort or another, and they sometimes culminate in the widely publicized execution of accused offenders after show trials.

Ivan and Anna Ivanov must accept not only the number of goods offered to them but also the quality. For various reasons inherent in the economic system, goods are generally of poor quality by Western standards. Even though consumers would be willing to pay more for better wares, they have no way of doing so. Some effort has been made within the last few years, in connection with a program of selective economic reforms, to make production more responsive to consumer demand at least in regard to quality, but the situation has improved only slightly.

When all is said, it is the difference between capitalism, on the one hand, and state socialism, on the other, that explains why John Doe has the right to pursue his own happiness while Ivan Ivanov does not. Private property is simply the other side of the coin to liberty. It is the means, and pragmatically the only means, whereby power may be dispersed within a society. Combined with competitive enterprise, it enables commands from the top to be replaced by voluntary exchange in the marketplace, so that the ordinary citizen may exercise free choice in mapping out the course of his life. Of course, liberty means little if the power to act is absent, but the state need not destroy freedom of choice in order to redistribute property.

By abolishing private property, the Soviet state has become the sole owner of all resources except personal effects, and therefore the master of every citizen's fate. Ivan can turn nowhere else to earn his livelihood, to find a place to live, to get his daily bread, to become educated, and to provide for the future. He is wholly at his masters' mercy.

Freedom of choice does not ensure either an easy or comfortable life. Some people may even be tempted to enslave themselves to avoid the tedium of making decisions and seeking a livelihood. But few slaves find their lot happy compared to that of the free man, as the world would see if Ivan and his compatriots were allowed to vote with their feet.

VIII

Creative Diversity

A prominent businessman who had risen from rags to riches was once asked whether he had any words of advice for young men on how to get ahead. "Yes," he replied, "they should work hard and submit to the rigors of the profit system. They should do as I do: buy for one dollar, sell for two, and make their one percent."

Many people are no doubt enticed into business by such rosy dreams of success, but few manage to realize them. It is the profit motive that makes our economy go, but the competitive seeking after profit may cause it to vanish or even to change into loss. Although profit is the lure, it usually eludes the grasp.

Our economy is most accurately characterized as a free enterprise system in which a vast multitude of firms undertake an enormous variety of business ventures. Those who bear the risks of these ventures are the entrepreneurs, and they are the ones who capture the profits or suffer the losses corresponding to success or failure.

In a complex market economy such as ours, enterprises play the central role of undertaking activities in response to consumer demands within an atmosphere of constantly altering tastes, technology, and resources. Decisions on what to pay for resources and how to use them must be made now on the basis of guesses about the availability of resources, the state of industrial arts, and the marketability of products at some future time. The affluence, progress, and diversity of our economy are living tributes to the efficiency of the free enterprise system in making these speculative judgments.

The prospect of rich rewards stimulates private initiative and encourages venturesome behavior. At the same time, the discipline of losses serves to restrain recklessness and to enforce efficiency. Creative drives are mobilized for the benefit of the individual consumer. Even the smallest potential markets do not escape the watchful eye of entrepreneurs in search of profits. The hallmark of our economy is creative diversity.

We should be clear about one thing: Free enterprise means the right of anybody to engage in a business, not the right of an existing firm to do anything it pleases. To promote freedom of entry, policies against monopolization and restraint of trade have long occupied an important place in the American tradition. It would be foolhardy to expect all traces of monopoly to be eliminated from a market economy, and studies indicate that perhaps a fifth of the total production in this country occurs under varying degrees of monopolistic control. But despite assertions to the contrary, particularly on the part of Marxists, the evidence shows no discernible growth in the extent of monopoly since at least the turn of the century. Our economy is and has been predominantly competitive.

While the intense competitive spirit driving our economy may bring with it conduct that seems undesirable in some respects, it provides at the same time a mighty engine of progress and innovation consonant with individual liberty. As the great English economist Alfred Marshall once noted, our system has the virtue of harnessing the strongest, if not the highest, motives of mankind for its benefit rather than harm. It has surely been better to channel the competitive spirit into productive activity within a regime of free enterprise and dispersed power than to let it assert itself in a political struggle for dominance over fellow men such as we observe in the Soviet Union.

Our system makes it possible for John Doe to serve the welfare of others by pursuing his own interests. By responding to the incentive to improve his own lot, he will be drawn generally to seek out those employments of his labor and property that are worth most to others. The system will not work unless some disparities in income and wealth are tolerated, but this does not mean that any degree of inequality in material well-being is justifiable. On the contrary, we have deliberately chosen to make the shares in our economic pie more equal even though that has made the pie smaller than it otherwise would have been.

We have probably gone too far in some respects. For example, the steeply graduated rates of taxation on higher levels of personal income sharply reduce incentives without yielding much revenue or providing a significant redistribution of income. The heavy and progressive taxes on corporate income are even more in point, for they inhibit venturesome and productive activity while bringing about quite mixed effects on income distribution. We must remember that there are more stockholders in our country, drawn from a wide range of income classes than there are members of labor unions.

While American society thrives on private initiative, the Soviet economy stifles under the dead weight of bureaucratic controls. The effort to direct everything from the center in accord with a master plan mapping the course of the future makes innovation a disruptive force. Since the system is so cumbersome and inflexible, the search for new ways of doing things or novel products to be produced is bound to be discouraged at all levels. The Soviet counterparts of the entrepreneurs of our society are bureaucratic managers preoccupied with the organization of routine tasks set from above.

These managers have little to gain and a great deal to lose from venturesome activity. If they succeed in making the economic units under their supervision function better, they may merely find heavier burdens imposed on themselves. If their innovations misfire, on the other hand, and cause planned goals to be undershot, they will be punished in one way or another. Not too long ago, they might be accused of economic sabotage and be imprisoned or executed. Even now they may suffer a wrecked career.

Since nobody has any fully transferable rights to private property, rewards are not adequately linked to personal effort, and there is little incentive for individual initiative. Encouragement of explorative behavior is confined largely to the realm of basic scientific research and special areas, such as the military, that are directly related to the power of the state. Elsewhere the wisest course is to play it safe.

Another important aspect of this system is the regime of austerity imposed on the populace. The wares Ivan may buy are sparse in number, standardized in form, and generally poor in quality. Very few of the multitudinous personal services found in economies catering to consumer sovereignty are offered to him. Such a lack of variety, style, and individuality is common to socialist economies that try to control everything from above. The rulers of the Soviet Union make it worse by their obsession with the sheer quantitative performance of the economy. Although conditions have noticeably improved recently, in part because better and more stylish consumer goods are being imported, life remains on the whole drab for the Ivanovs.

These faults rest with the Soviet system and not the people, who are as able, energetic, and imaginative as any in the world. If consumers were sovereign in the Soviet Union, they would demand the same things of their economy as others do. If private enterprise were allowed, the economy would respond as elsewhere to those demands by producing what consumers want.

Within the severe restraints placed upon them, Soviet plant managers are highly efficient, and many of them would be excellent entrepreneurs if they had the opportunity. Some entrepreneurial talent is mobilized by plant managers to get their "pushers," who scurry about seeking ways of acquiring needed materials outside the rigid system of centralized allocation. Some find its way into the complex maze of black and gray markets.

Such activities, now misused in circumventing an inflexible system, show that risk-bearing skill remains plentiful, just as the solid achievements of Soviet science clearly demonstrate the inherent creative genius of the people. These talents need merely to be unleashed to bring them to the service of the populace.

The one small island of legitimate activities that most closely resembles private enterprise in the Soviet Union is the work done by peasants on their tiny private plots. The peasant households may attend to these plots only in their spare time, after performing required duties on collective or state farms, but the incentive of being allowed to enjoy the fruits of their own labor brings forth intense effort. The results are remarkable: Although the private plots account for only 3 percent of the total cultivated area, they produce about 30 percent of the food supply. This crop is consumed by the peasants growing it or sold by them for cash in special urban marketplaces.

The frustrations of the system help to generate a defensive mentality that often takes the form of an inverted inferiority complex. One of the many imaginary stories in this vein has to do with the visit of an American tourist to a technological museum. Many of the great inventions of the Industrial Age were on display: the telephone, radio, the internal combustion engine, jet propulsion, the computer, and so on. Before each stood a little sign: "Invented by Plotnikov, the great Russian scientist." The American was finally moved to remark to his guide that Plotnikov must indeed be the greatest of all Russian inventors.

"Oh, no," replied the guide, "He is our second greatest inventor. Petrov is the greatest."

"But," the American protested, "if Plotnikov was responsible for all these marvelous inventions, what in the world did Petrov invent?"

"That is quite simple," the guide answered. "Petrov invented Plotnikov."

The stifling of individuality and creative diversity in economic relations is but a manifestation of the atmosphere of conformity that overhangs Soviet society as a whole. The authoritarian and totalitarian regime, while bowing formally to the principle of cultural self-determination, is fundamentally at odds with the reality of a heterogeneous society.

The fate of minorities under Communism may be illustrated by the way in which the so-called "nationalities problem" has been handled. One of the most notorious imperial powers of all time, Russia was formed over the centuries by a steady policy of expansion implemented primarily by the conquest of neighboring peoples and nations. The Soviet leadership, experiencing a frightening disintegration of the country after the Bolshevik Revolution, reconstituted the empire by force of arms and proclaimed it to be a voluntary union of socialist republics. The nationalities problem has remained unresolved, as the official policy of molding a homogeneous society, based largely on the Great Russian culture, has met constant resistance from the separate ethnic groups.

The contrast in historical roots between the Soviet Union and the United States is obvious. Our motto, "e Pluribus Unum" or "one out of many," means more than the joining together of many states to form a nation. It also means the amalgamation of many races, colors, and creeds into a single person. Our country was settled by migrants from a great variety of cultures and nations, many seeking a haven from oppression. They came here mainly to lose one national identity and find another, and they thrust themselves into what came to be known as a great melting pot. While they and their progeny might take pride in their national origins, they have considered themselves Americans by nationality as well as citizenship, even though they might on occasion refer to themselves in hyphenated terms.

The distinction between nationality and citizenship is taken much more seriously in the Soviet Union by authorities as well as individuals. This is not to say that it is easy to define what is meant by nationality. According to the classic definition of Joseph Stalin, a nationality must have a common culture consisting of a language, territory, economic life, and psychological make-up. But these abstract criteria are seldom strictly applied even when they can be given concrete meaning. Instead, Ivan is assigned the nationality of his parents, just as they were assigned that of theirs back as far as one wishes to go. This is the method normally used to resolve questions of racial or ethnic origin whenever a government insists on recording it. If Ivan comes from "mixed" parentage, he presumably may choose which nationality he is to bear.

If he lives in a city, Ivan must declare his nationality at the age of sixteen when he first applies for his domestic passport. The label then attached to him will stick for the rest of his life. Such permanent identification is important because it enables the state to implement discriminatory practices against a minority at any time that it may wish to do so.

During World War II, seven nationality groups in the Soviet Union were uprooted from their ancient homelands, deported to remote areas, and dispersed in scattered settlements. About a million and a half people were removed from homes extending over an area a third as large as the state of Pennsylvania, a region then opened to settlement by favored Russians and Ukrainians. Perhaps as many as 40 percent of the deportees died during the cruel journey by cattle trucks from Western Russia into various parts of Siberia.

It was not until 1956, when Khrushchev made his famous speech denouncing Stalin, that the enormity of this act was made public. After discussing some of the deportations, Khrushchev said: "Not only no Marxist-Leninist but also no man of common sense can grasp how it is possible to make whole nations responsible for inimical activity, including women, children, old people, Communists and Komsomols [Young Communists], to use mass repression against them, and to expose them to misery and suffering for the hostile acts of individual persons or groups of persons."[15]

So much for the condemnation after the fact. The fact itself remains as evidence of what could then and might once again be done by the authoritarian Soviet state.

Evidence came to light in 1968 of a trial of twenty Ukrainians that was secretly held at about the time of the celebrated Sinyavsky-Daniel case. All were young intellectuals, mainly with academic posts. Their trial is described in an account smuggled to the West and written by a young Ukrainian journalist, Vyacheslav Chornovil, who was sentenced to eighteen months in a labor camp for protesting the treatment of the twenty.

Chornovil writes that the intellectuals "were charged with anti-Soviet nationalistic propaganda and agitation and some also with 'organizational activity.' However, even those from whom repentance had been forced after long months refused to admit at the trials that they had read 'forbidden' books or articles to 'undermine or weaken the Soviet order.'"

---

15 Chornovil manuscript cited in *The New York Times*. 1968. Feb. 9, 2.

The "crime" with which these Ukrainian scholars were charged was the study of their cultural heritage with a view to understanding and cultivating it. This was anti-Soviet conduct. They were punished accordingly: One was banished, and fifteen were sentenced to terms of up to six years in concentration camps.

Persecution of the Jews is an example of how a minority may be persistently mistreated as a matter of official policy. The Jews continue to be designated as a nationality even though they exhibit few of the characteristics officially associated with one: only a small fraction (perhaps a quarter) speak Yiddish as a native tongue, an even smaller fraction actively practice the Jewish religion, and only some 14,000 are congregated in a separate territorial unit allegedly intended for Jews.

By official count, there are over two million Soviet Jews. The state permits them to have a total of 60 synagogues. By contrast, there are 5,500 churches for the half-million Baptists. No seminary is permitted for the training of rabbis, and no rabbis may study abroad. None were permitted even to travel abroad until June 1968, when a rabbi and a cantor were authorized to make a two-week trip to the United States. The existing congregations are not allowed to confederate in a national organization. Not since 1958, when 3,000 copies of a prayer book were issued, has any religious publication been permitted. There can be little doubt that the Jewish religion is persecuted beyond all others of any size in the Soviet Union.

The official policy carries over into the realm of culture. Although there are many schools for other linguistic minorities—including some tiny ones—in which classes are conducted in native languages, the privilege to use either Yiddish or Hebrew is not accorded in a single school throughout the Soviet Union. The Yiddish theater, which once flourished, has long been closed, and a formerly rich literature has all but vanished.

To a people with such a strong tradition of learning, the recent tightening of the quota for admission of Jews to higher education down to 3 percent is especially harsh. Similar discrimination has become increasingly apparent in declining opportunities to enter certain professions and to rise to prominent positions. For example, almost 11 percent of the Central Committee of the Communist Party were Jews in 1939 as compared with less than one-third of 1 percent today, or one Jewish member out of 360. The situation is roughly the same for the Supreme Soviet.

Hovering over this undeniable set of discriminatory policies is the ugly specter of official anti-Semitism, always veiled but nonetheless real. In the campaign against so-called "economic crimes" carried out in the early 1960s, more than half of those who were publicly announced as having been executed bore conspicuously Jewish names. In Ukraine, the fraction was 90 percent, even though Jews constitute only 2 percent of the population.

Anti-Semitism as an official policy has virtually leaped into the open in the aftermath of the Arab-Israeli war of 1967. Through that curious inversion of logic not uncommon to Communist propaganda, the Israelis have been accused of behaving like Nazis. The newspaper of the Young Communist League has provided the ultimate twist in defense of this curious analogy by accusing "Zionists" of deliberately fomenting anti-Semitism for their own benefit. This accusation is made in an article containing all the invective typical of a racist diatribe.

We could go on documenting at length the mistreatment of the Jewish minority in the Soviet Union, but we have said enough to make the basic point. What is perhaps more important is that the same thing can happen at any time to other identifiable ethnic or racial groups incurring the displeasure of the state.

The persecution at issue here is a matter of official policy, enforced by the power of the state. There is no society on earth, certainly including our own, in which minorities do not suffer simply because they differ from the bulk of the population in some way considered significant and undesirable. They will be discriminated against, and the roots of such discrimination lie in concrete personal attitudes of members of the dominant group, not in the abstract mentality of some collectivity. Discrimination may be practiced by individuals in private affairs or by governmental authorities in political relations, and the latter is always more pernicious than the former. In any case, it is vain to expect private manifestations of prejudice to vanish until we enter a golden age of angels on earth.

Since we are bound to be most familiar with the many unsavory conditions close to home, we should become aware of the fact that racial prejudices are also deeply ingrained in Soviet life. It has been almost 500 years since the Russians threw off the Mongol and Tatar yoke that had kept them in subservience for more than two centuries, but the antagonism between Slav and Oriental remains. There is a popular basis for the Sino-Soviet conflict of today.

By contrast, there was very little contact in early times between the peoples of Russia and Africa, and no more than a handful of Negroes live in the Soviet Union today. Yet prejudice against the Negro quickly rose to the surface when relatively large numbers of African students began to be admitted to Soviet universities during the present decade. Difficulties have arisen despite an official policy of affording special privileges to these students, and they have twice erupted into serious disturbances. In each case, an African student was murdered after mixing socially with Russian girls. Many of the African students have returned home in a disgruntled and resentful mood, and they have complained openly about the discriminatory treatment they experienced.

In the world of practical alternatives, the important question to raise in judging a society is not whether there is prejudice but whether there are means of escaping it. Minorities may expect to fare better in the United States than in the Soviet Union for two reasons: first, because they are not oppressed as a matter of national policy; and, second, because the escape route of the market is open to them.

The latter point is vividly illustrated by Milton Friedman, the eminent economist, in his book *Capitalism and Freedom*:

It is a striking historical fact that the development of capitalism has been accompanied by a major reduction in the extent to which particular religious, racial, or social groups have operated under special handicaps in respect of their economic activities; have, as the saying goes, been discriminated against. The substitution of contract arrangements for status arrangements was the first step toward the freeing of the serfs in the Middle Ages. The preservation of Jews through the Middle Ages was possible because of the existence of a market sector in which they could operate and maintain themselves despite official persecution. Puritans and Quakers were able to migrate to the New World because they could accumulate the funds to do so in the market despite disabilities imposed on them in other aspects of their life. The Southern states after the Civil War took many measures to impose legal restrictions on Negroes. One measure which was never taken on any scale was the establishment of barriers to the ownership of either real or personal property. The failure to impose such barriers clearly did not reflect any special concern to avoid restrictions on Negroes. It reflected, rather, a basic belief in private property which was so strong that it overrode the desire to discriminate against Negroes. The maintenance of the general rules of private property and of capitalism have been a major source of opportunity for Negroes and have permitted them to make greater progress than they otherwise would have made. To take a more general example, the preserves of discrimination in any society are the areas that are most monopolistic in character, whereas discrimination against groups of particular color or religion is least in those areas where there is the greatest freedom of competition.[16]

In other words, the marketplace is color blind. When the family head shops for a new television set, he asks about its quality and price, but not about what color the hands were that assembled it. When a person applies for a loan at the bank, he wants to know the interest rate, but not the religion or ethnic background of the lender.

This is not to say that unfair discrimination is absent in the choice of customers or employees—on the part of fellow shoppers and workers as well as bosses. But competition means that there will be many alternative places to work and shop, and the search for profits will lead some entrepreneurs to employ and cater to those who suffer unfair discrimination elsewhere. Moreover, the opportunity is always open to going into business for one's self in an economy based on private property and free enterprise.

Where may a Soviet citizen turn who is oppressed by reason of race,

16 Friedman, M. 1962. *Capitalism and Freedom*. Chicago: The University of Chicago Press, 108-109.

color, or creed? There is only one legal employer: the state. Except for food, he has only one legal place to shop: the state stores. He has only one landlord to whom he can apply for housing: the state. The state schools provide his sole opportunity for education. And so on and on. How can minorities escape persecution by the all-powerful state? Only by turning to the generally illicit marketplaces, and then they must live the dangerous life of outlaws.

All the sputniks, missiles, and mausoleums in the world will not make up for the intolerance of Soviet life. The greatness of a society does not come from its monuments but from the kind of people it produces. Justice, tolerance, responsibility, individuality, and humanity—these are the qualities of greatness in a person. We know that only the humane can remain free. But it is equally true that only the free will remain humane.

IX

The General Welfare

During the Middle Ages, what the educated few in the West knew about the Orient came mainly from the writings of a Venetian traveler, Marco Polo. Today, our vision of life in the Soviet Union is perhaps also based on travelers' tales as much as anything else, for Soviet rulers are nowhere more secretive than on matters relating to the living conditions of the masses. The rulers permit only sketchy and misleading statistics to see the light of day.

Yet the published statistics are sufficient to contradict the reports of casual visitors who are understandably impressed by officially guided tours and staged interviews. Two examples may be drawn from a series of articles in *The New York Times* written on the occasion of the fiftieth anniversary of the Bolshevik Revolution in 1967.

In one, the author writes in glowing terms of the rapid progress being made in overcoming the perennial housing shortage. Special praise is given to the program for constructing large apartment buildings out of prefabricated concrete panels that are mass-produced off the site. This method is said to be, among other things, cheaper and technologically superior to any construction technique employed in the United States.

From her conducted inspection of sites, the author could not, of course, have been aware of how little new housing is being provided in this way or of how shoddy much of the resulting construction has been. During the four years ending in 1965, this technique accounted for only some 6 percent of additional floor space according to official figures. After a careful study of basic sources, Timothy Sosnovy, the foremost expert on Soviet housing in this country, concludes that "Soviet officials are particularly concerned with the inefficiencies and substandard quality of large-panel construction." He points out that many enterprises have "produced parts of completely unsatisfactory quality, with a low degree of factory readiness. As a result, many apartment buildings are constructed and operated with numerous defects."

He goes on to say: "In some cases the situation is evidently even worse. For example, during 1961–63, 42 five-floor apartment houses were constructed in Kiev, with a total floor space of 104,000 square meters. In view of the low quality of the structural materials used, progressive cracks began to appear in the external wall panels, and further construction of these buildings had to be suspended."[17]

In another article in the same New York Times series, a second commentator writes about the way people live. She quotes a number of women with whom she spoke and whose homes she visited during her brief tour. They include an executive of the Moscow Subway Construction Agency, an official of the All-Union Council of Trade Unions, a professor of Moscow State University, the manager of a hotel in Moscow, the wife of a famous composer, an eminent lawyer, a high government official from Georgia, a prominent surgeon, a leading poetess, a rising ballerina—all members of the very upper crust of Soviet society. They represent at most the top 5 percent of the population, and we can learn little from their sheltered lives about the trials and tribulations of the masses.

The fact is that almost no outsider really knows how the average man lives in Russia. The visitor is likely, in the first place, to see only the big cities where the living standard is highest, starting from Moscow and moving downward through Leningrad, Kiev, and so on, roughly in order of population. Even if he carefully tours all the largest cities, he will not sample the life of more than a tenth of the population.

---

17 Sosnovy, T. in *New Directions in the Soviet Economy*. 1966. Joint Economic Committee. Washington: Governmemnt Printing Office, II, 543.

Moreover, he has virtually no way of making contact with ordinary people, since official policy strongly discourages mixing with foreigners. It is not a question of physical barriers alone. The people do not respond openly to friendly overtures, for they know that fraternization with foreigners can get them into serious political trouble.

The tourist who keeps his eyes open and wanders from the path beaten for him by official guides can, of course, get a glimpse of the more normal aspects of Soviet life. But it will be a rare person who manages to talk freely with an ordinary worker, and an even rarer one who sets foot in his home. As in the Russia of old, novels are often a better source of information about how people live than travelers' tales. And so are the official statistics, no matter how biased and fragmentary they may be.

Let us start with the cold figures on urban housing. The official statistics tell us that the amount of housing space per urban inhabitant is less than 70 square feet. On average, there are 2.3 persons living in each room. In this simple respect, urban housing is more crowded now than it was before the Revolution half a century ago. But conditions have improved considerably from the low point just before World War II, when average living space was around 45 square feet, or hardly more than double the size of a gravesite.

The average amount of urban housing space today is only 70 percent of the minimum sanitary norm set by the Soviet government more than a generation ago. Even if the urban population did not increase in the meantime, existing housing would have to be more than doubled in order to reach the ultimate goal of one person per room. And, since housing facilities are so unevenly distributed among the various classes of Soviet society, we must remember that half the urban residents live in even more crowded conditions than these figures show.

By normal international standards, it is considered excessive crowding to have more than one and a half persons per room. Probably less than one percent of the housing units in the United States are overcrowded in that sense. Only 12 percent had more than one person per room according to the census of 1960. Living space per person is around 350 square feet or 5 times the Soviet figure. It seems clear that the Ivanovs, our ordinary Soviet family, reside in what is considered a slum here.

This is even more apparent when we recognize that kitchen and bathroom facilities are, except for the privileged classes, shared by a number of families in Soviet apartment buildings. Even in the case of the newest apartments, about half have communal kitchens and bathrooms. And those fortunate enough to get one of these must normally have applied at least five years in advance.

Soviet apartments are not only overcrowded but also badly built. One observer has remarked that the Soviets have discovered the art of constructing old buildings from scratch. Normally, a building is scarcely erected before the walls develop gaping cracks, doorways sag, floors buckle, facades crumble, and stairways lean. Paradoxically, the sturdiest housing seems to be that was built in pre-Revolutionary days.

To put matters in perspective, let us listen to a description of how some of the better half live. It was written by Yury Krotkov in his book The Angry Exile published in 1967. Before his recent defection, Krotkov was a successful writer, and the Moscow apartment he describes contained about 100 square feet of living space per resident, or significantly more than the average in that city. He writes as follows:

Our apartment contained eleven rooms. It had one kitchen with eight gas-rings, three bells (one general, and two individual), a telephone in the corridor which was in constant use, a bath, and a lavatory, which only the fastest were able to get to in the morning (the others stopped in at the public lavatories on their way to work). There were eighteen people in the apartment, besides myself. Seven families, seven meters for electricity, seven tables and cupboards in the kitchen, and seven launderings a month, since none of my neighbors used the state laundries. This was not because they did not like them, but because they were economizing. There was not a single washing-machine in the apartment; we had never even heard of a clothes dryer. But there were three television sets and two radios. Furthermore, all eighteen people ate at home. They never went to even the cheapest cafeteria, much less a restaurant. Again, it was because of the expense. . . .

So my Moscow apartment was somewhat typical. But at the same time, we were exceptional, in that each resident generally could say with satisfaction: "It's crowded, but the people, thank the Lord, are decent. They don't spit in their neighbor's soup, as they do in Apartment 5."[18]

In the words of the author, these housing conditions are a luxury in the Moscow of today—except for the privileged classes, who live in the elegant villas of the rich of former times or in spacious apartments.

If we go back about a decade, the last date for which such data are available, we find that around 90 percent of the urban population was supplied with electricity, 34 percent with running water, 31 percent with plumbing, 22 percent with central heating, 16 percent with gas, 9 percent with a bath, and 2 percent with hot water. In the case of private homes, which housed about a quarter of the urban population, only 70 percent had electricity, one percent running water, and about one-third of one percent the other amenities.

For occupied units in the United States, rural as well as urban,

---

18 Krotkov, Y. 1967. *The Angry Exile*. London: William Heinemann Ltd., 125-127.

recent figures show that virtually all had electricity, 93 percent running water, 67 percent central heating, 94 percent gas, 81 percent a private bathroom, and 87 percent hot water.

Crowded housing conditions are not the only bad aspect of urban life in the Soviet Union. If we leave aside the specially favored cities, most streets are still dirt roads. In Novosibirsk, only 18 percent of the streets are paved, and in Sverdlovsk only 40 percent. Both have populations of almost a million. Water lines run less than half the length of city streets, and sewage lines less than half the length of water lines. Only about half the sewage and almost none of the industrial waste is treated before entering inland waterways, which are far more polluted than ours.

If this is the way things are in the city, how are they in the villages? One may only suppose that they are much the same as they always have been. The peasants still live in their huts and cottages, roomier than the apartments of the city but even less well provided with modern conveniences. Perhaps most have electricity, at least in the form of a light socket or two, and some will have a radio. But water will still be drawn mainly from the well, the toilet will be an outhouse, and heat will come from an oven, stove, or hearth. Life in the countryside remains primitive and miserable.

The standard of living of the average Soviet man is equally low in other respects. While Ivan's diet contains about as many calories as John Doe's, almost three-fifths come from starchy foods, instead of the one quarter here. In per capita consumption, the Soviet Union ranks behind only Egypt and Yugoslavia for bread and only Poland for potatoes. The purchase of food accounts for about three-fifths of the average Soviet budget as compared with one-fifth of the American.

Consumption of hard liquor is a rough inverse indicator of the standard of living, and alcoholism is a very serious problem in the Soviet Union. The average Russian drinks as much as the average American drank around a century or more ago—or three times as much as today's average American.

Everything considered, how well do the Ivanovs live relative to the Does? There are so many deficiencies in Soviet statistics and incomparabilities in conditions that it is extremely difficult to give a concise and meaningful answer to this question. Our own governmental agencies, such as the Central Intelligence Agency, estimate the typical standard of living in the Soviet Union to be about 30 percent of the level in this country, but this figure seems to be much too high. We may see why by looking at average incomes in the two countries.

If we leave aside differences in the quality and availability of products, the ruble would seem to have about the same overall purchasing power as the dollar when considered in terms of a pattern of consumption roughly intermediate between those of the two countries. The earnings of the average wage or salary worker in the Soviet Union, as given by official statistics, then translate into about

$1,200 a year. On the average, each family has, again according to official statistics, 1.6 breadwinners. Hence, the annual income for a typical family outside of collectivized agriculture would run to $1,900. For the peasant household, representing about two-fifths of the population, the appropriate figure would be hardly more than half as large.

A reasonable estimate of the average family income would, therefore, be about $1,500 a year, or half the standard set by our present administration as the "poverty level" for Americans. Because incomes are quite unequally distributed, this average is no doubt significantly higher than the median, or the income enjoyed by half or less of the families.

The current median annual income for American families is $7,400. Comparing the figures for the two countries, we find the Does to be about five times as well off as the Ivanovs. Such a comparison is not entirely satisfactory, however, because it leaves out of account possibly significant differences for the two countries in the share of income that must be deducted for payment of direct taxes, on the one hand, or added for receipt of "social benefits," on the other.

Interestingly enough, even though the personal income tax has much more steeply graduated rates in the United States than in the Soviet Union, the fraction of income paid in taxes by the average family is somewhat lower here than there. In the case of so-called "social benefits," Soviet statisticians state that more than a third should be added to the earnings of the typical nonagricultural worker to make allowance for such things as free education, health care, and other services for which no charges are made. It is impossible to know how meaningful these calculations are, and in any case a broad range of such social services is also provided in this country by government and charitable institutions. Perhaps they are relatively more significant in the Soviet Union, but their importance would seem to be at least fully offset by the higher quality of goods and services of all kinds consumed in the United States.

All things considered, the ratio of 5 to 1 is a reasonable estimate of the superiority of our standard of living over the Soviet one, with an exception to be noted in a moment. The gap becomes even larger when we weigh the factor of freedom of consumer choice.

Relative per capita consumption in the two countries varies enormously among different goods and services. In a comprehensive study made by one of our governmental agencies of conditions in 1955, Soviet per capita consumption was found to be three-tenths of one percent of ours for automobiles and gasoline, 4 percent for personal services, 9 percent for household appliances, 16 percent for housing and related amenities, 17 percent for textiles and wearing apparel, 25 percent for meat and canned goods, 29 percent for vegetables and fruits, 49 percent for sugar and confections, 52 percent for health and educational services, 108 percent for public transportation, 162 percent for cereal products and potatoes, and almost 300 percent for alcoholic beverages.

To enjoy a standard of living about a fifth of ours, the Soviet Union employs a labor force one and a half times as large. The workforce constitutes 75 percent of the adult population there as compared with 57 percent here. In the case of women, the respective figures are 50 percent and 37 percent. To purchase a basket of food intermediate between United States and Soviet standards, a wage earner in Moscow must work about 8 times as long as one in New York City.

The disparity in living standards for John Doe and Ivan Ivanov is even greater than all these figures show, for they leave out of account the important element of consumption within the household economy. The normal American family is so accustomed to its vast array of personal capital goods, yielding so many services in the household, that it can hardly imagine how poor Ivan is in this respect. In the Soviet Union, the number of privately owned automobiles is about 2 per thousand inhabitants or one for every 135 families. In the United States, the figure is 400 per thousand or 1.4 per family. In rounded figures, the stocks of other consumer durables per thousand persons are as follows for the Soviet Union and the United States, respectively: radios, 170 and 980; television sets, 70 and 330; telephones, 30 and 480; refrigerators, 30 and 290; washing machines, 50 and 220; and vacuum cleaners, 20 and 210. The stocks range from 5 to 200 times as large in the United States as in the Soviet Union.

The primitive state of household conveniences and market facilities means that Ivan and Anna Ivanov must spend most of their leisure time in shopping and performing household chores. Official surveys indicate that at least 70 percent of free time is spent in these ways, much of it standing in queues one place or another. In the usual store, Ivan must wait in three lines: to select his goods, to pay for them, and to pick them up. The recent opening of a pick-up and delivery service for a Moscow laundry was considered so noteworthy that it warranted a proud announcement in the press.

The packaging of consumer goods is almost unknown. For example, only 1 percent of the butter sold is packaged, 2 percent of the meat, and 7 percent of the sugar and macaroni products.

Despite the poor quality of consumer products, there are only 4 repair shops of all types for every 10,000 inhabitants. Per capita expenditures on repairs run less than $5 a year. An article in the Soviet press in 1968 indicates that half or more of certain brands of television sets stop working shortly after they are purchased. Yet one repair shop had only 32 technicians to service 82,000 sets, and they could handle 250 calls a day at most.

To turn to another aspect of economic life, we may note once again that there is at least as large a disparity in incomes among members of the working class in the Soviet Union as in the United States. As far as town and country are concerned, one prominent

Soviet economist, A G. Aganbegian, has remarked that "under existing conditions, if the people were allowed to leave the countryside hardly anyone would remain behind."[19] While there is no wealthy propertied class as such, the top political leaders surely have as sweeping a command over the comforts of life as millionaires in this country.

Aid to the indigent, infirm, incompetent, and aged must come from the Soviet government. There is no organized private charity— it is forbidden. The few specially licensed organizations like the Red Cross serve for all practical purposes as organs of the state.

There is a comprehensive program of socialized medicine providing health care without charge. Medical skills are generally of a lower quality than we are accustomed to, and the variety of services available is much less extensive, but these deficiencies are balanced by a larger medical staff relative to the population. In the field of public health and preventive medicine, an efficient job is done.

There is a system of social security providing pensions for retired workers. Until about a decade ago, retirement benefits were shockingly low, but since then they have risen significantly. They remain, of course, very small by our standards. Until 1964, members of collective farms were not covered, and even now their pensions

---

19 Aganbegian, A. 1965. *The ASTE Bulletin*, Summer.

are far lower than those for wage earners, while eligibility requirements are much stiffer. For instance, the minimum full monthly
pension is 12 rubles for a collective farmer as compared with 30
for a wage earner.

There is no unemployment insurance because everybody
is required to work and supposedly guaranteed a job. Since the
government proclaimed the abolition of all unemployment long
ago, it can hardly be expected to contradict itself by providing
unemployment benefits. Their absence imposes a serious hardship
on the relatively large number of persons who are in fact out of
work at any moment.

Ivan's lot is indeed not an easy one. By our standards, he lives in
a slum and enjoys a standard of life only halfway up to the poverty
line. John Doe has many material blessings to count.

X

Prosperity and Progress

Fiction has it that, somewhere in the depths of Armenia, there is a Radio Yerevan with a consistent record of political miscues in its broadcasts. On one occasion, so the tale runs, the chief political commentator committed suicide rather than announce over the air two statements sent down from Moscow.

The first said that the American capitalist economy was teetering precariously on the brink of a precipice and would at any moment plunge downward to be smashed to bits; the second, that the Soviet Union was about to overtake and surpass the United States in economic performance.

The golden promise that their economy would soon rush past

ours has been held up to the Soviet people by their rulers almost from the moment of the Revolution. The event is usually predicted for a decade hence. And, as the decades roll by, it seems to remain as remote as ever. The Soviet masses have long since learned to greet this propaganda with weary indifference.

This has not always been true of observers in the West, however. Deeply impressed by Soviet claims of economic growth and even more so by achievements in the space program, many American experts came to view the Soviet economy as a miraculous engine of expansion able to generate rates of growth unprecedented in history. As recently as five or six years ago, crossover points—when Soviet industrial output would begin to exceed ours–were still being forecast for the early 1970s.

Similar views permeated thinking in government circles. In 1958, shortly after the first sputnik was launched, Allen Dulles, then director of the CIA, characterized normal Soviet growth rates as having "rarely been matched in other states except during limited periods of postwar rebuilding."[20] A year later, he predicted that "Soviet GNP [gross national product] will grow at the rate of 6 percent a year through 1965."[21]

In fact, Soviet economic growth was already slowing down

----

20 Dulles quoted in *The New York Times*. 1958. April 29, 8.

21 Dulles quoted in *Hearings*. 1959. Joint Economic Committee. November, 9.

sharply when these words were uttered, and the prediction did not come true. The spectacular crop failure of 1963 finally called attention to what was happening. A number of academic experts were quoted in the press as expressing incredulity when informed in January 1964 of a CIA estimate that growth of the Soviet economy had slipped to 2.5 percent a year in 1962 and 1963.

This episode would seem to demonstrate that American specialists had, by and large, concluded that the Soviet economy was superior to Western economies in creating growth.

The fact is that there was little in the historical record to warrant such a sense of awe toward Soviet economic performance. Western experts will argue among themselves over the accuracy of precise rates of growth and the interpretations to be placed on them, as we should expect when Soviet data are so ambiguous and incomplete. But, when all is said, their calculations seem to point to the same conclusion: The Soviet economy has grown no faster over its fifty years of life than our own. True enough, there have been spectacular spurts of growth over short periods of time, but they have left little imprint on long-run performance.

Looked at the other way around, Soviet performance in terms of sheer quantitative growth is just as impressive as ours, and in that respect, full credit must be given. However, from this point on, the resemblance between the expansion paths of the two economies fades away.

Our economic development has swept across all sectors and emphasized the continual enhancement of consumer welfare. Theirs has focused on the growth of industry and aggrandizement of national power. Ours has come mainly from innovation and improved efficiency in the use of resources, theirs from expanded employment of resources.

An economy run by centralized planning makes headway quickly by concentrating on easy tasks and neglecting difficult ones. Through a process of natural selection, the growth targets that get fulfilled or overfulfilled are those most easily met. If the primary aim is to strengthen military and political power as rapidly as possible, industrialization gets pressed forward at the expense of almost everything else, including those parts of the industry that do not directly implement power.

Preoccupation with a high rate of measured economic growth, largely for the sake of propaganda, has much the same effect. Production becomes an end in itself as sight is lost of the basic reason for an economy.

Following this course, the Soviet economy has become more and more burdened with problems too long postponed. An economic system always too busy and clumsy to deal with problems as they arose now faces the real danger of simply breaking down under their accumulated weight.

The Soviet economy produces a great deal, though probably

not so much as some popular estimates imply. Our government agencies tell us that the Soviet gross national product is now more than two fifths as large as ours, but a more meaningful figure would be around a third.

Private consumption accounts for less than half of the total GNP there as compared with almost two thirds here. On the other side of the coin, gross investment accounts for almost a third in the Soviet case as compared with about a fifth in ours. If the two economies were equally efficient, the much heavier rate of investment in the Soviet Union should lead to a consistently higher growth rate. Yet this is not the case.

The contrast in inefficiency is perhaps most striking in agriculture. Using a labor force more than 9 times the size of ours, the Soviet Union manages to produce an output of only 70 to 80 percent as large. By a generous interpretation, output per worker in Soviet agriculture can hardly be more than a twelfth of the American level. Moreover, while agriculture has one of the most rapid rates of increase in labor productivity in the United States, it has one of the slowest in the Soviet Union.

These almost incredible differences in performance are traceable to the inefficiencies of collectivized as opposed to private farming, and to the relatively starved condition of Soviet agriculture as far as capital equipment is concerned. For example, there are about 100 acres of arable land for every tractor in the United States as compared with 400 in the Soviet Union, and a large fraction of Soviet tractors are not in running order at any given moment.

Before the Revolution, Russia was a net exporter of food. Today, it is a net importer. A listener is said to have submitted the following query to the question-and-answer period of Radio Yerevan: "Is it true that all countries of the world will turn socialist?" The answer: "No, that is not true. For then, where would we buy our food?"

In the case of industry, the Soviet economy performs considerably better. Our government estimates current Soviet industrial production to be about half the level in this country, and once again this figure seems to be too high. To put it at a third would seem to be more reasonable. In any case, the Soviet Union employs 40 percent more industrial workers, in full-time equivalents, than we do. Hence the output per worker there would seem to be a fourth as large as here. This relative performance is about what it was before the Revolution, but it is far better than the one for agriculture.

The strain of coping with the normal array of problems does not deter the Soviet rulers from attending to the matter with top priority: production of military and space items. There is no more closely guarded secret than the size of that program, but from indirect evidence we may suppose that it is roughly equivalent to ours. The burden imposed on the Soviet economy is, however, three times as great as here. The message spelled out clearly by history is that economic strength is a poor gauge of military power, and vice versa.

During an air raid on Moscow in World War II, a Western military aide watched an anti-aircraft battery in action, fascinated by the accuracy of the guns and the skill with which they were handled. When the raid ended, he took out his pipe, filled it, and broke a dozen matches trying to light it. He hurled the box of matches to the ground and exclaimed to his companion, "How can people who make and man guns like those produce matches like these?"

In what sense can we say that the Soviet Union is prospering and progressing? Whom is the economic growth, purchased at such a high cost, benefiting? Certainly not Ivan Ivanov, whose standard of living creeps upward at a much slower pace than the output of the economy. In the last analysis, economic growth feeds the power of the state and its ruling elite.

It is a basic article of the Communist faith that economic fluctuations are to disappear under state socialism. Output is always to move smoothly upward, and unemployment is to vanish. There are to be none of the ups and downs characteristic of capitalist economies. In practice, any resemblance the Soviet economy may bear to this idyllic picture is quite superficial.

Every economy is subject to important and unpredictable disturbances from time to time, and responses to them inevitably involve curtailment of activities in some directions and expansion in others. It takes time to shift resources around from one use to another, and in the interim, there must be productive losses somewhere.

In a private enterprise economy such as ours, firms will respond to a fall in demand by reducing output and employment as quickly as possible. If the underlying disturbances are widespread, the result will be a recession in the economy as a whole before the slack can be taken up by countervailing expansion.

In the Soviet Union, the adjustment process takes a different form. Commodities may continue to be produced by plants, and workers employed producing them, even though there is no use for the commodities. Stocks of unwanted goods pile up until higher authorities finally undertake corrective action. Losses appear as accumulations of useless inventories rather than as reductions in output and employment. The cost in real income is nevertheless real, and it may exceed that in a capitalist economy if adjustments are unduly postponed.

Despite persistent official denials, unemployment itself is a significant and growing problem in the Soviet Union. When Soviet authorities say that there is no unemployment. they mean that there is a job somewhere for every worker. In principle, it does not matter that the jobs are, say, in Eastern Siberia while those out of work live in Moscow. Nor does it matter that the vacant jobs have lower wages and require lesser skills than the unemployed are qualified for. All that matters is that the number of jobs is equal to the number of able-bodied workers.

Since workers outside of agriculture have been permitted to quit their jobs, the rate at which jobs turn over has risen sharply. Annual rates of 22 to 30 percent have been reported as common, with a range of up to 90 percent. A recent study by a Soviet academician reveals a net migration of workers out of Siberia despite intensive recruitment efforts. Such heavy movements of labor are bound to produce high rates of frictional unemployment because it takes time for a worker to shift from one job to another. Meanwhile, he is out of work.

Professor Abel G. Aganbegian, whom we shall quote at greater length in a moment, commented on this question in 1965:

> At present, the employment problem (spoken of in the West as the unemployment problem) is very strongly felt here. Jobs must be created for 10,000,000 young people in the next five years. At the same time, one finds that there has been an increase in the number of persons without work during the past two years. This phenomenon occurs above all in small and medium-sized cities. On average 25 to 30 percent of the population able to work fails to find any employment in these cities. In the large cities, the figure... is 8 percent.[22]

Beset with a host of problems beyond its ability to resolve, the

22 Agenbegian, A. 1965. *The ASTE Bulletin*, Summer.

Soviet economy is, without exaggeration, faced with a crisis. The nature of that crisis is nowhere better indicated than in a speech given less than three years ago by Professor Aganbegian, a brilliant young economist and director of an important economic institute in Siberia. The speech was widely circulated as an unpublished manuscript in the Soviet Union and later published in the West. In part, it reads as follows:

> During the past six years, the rate of development of our economy has decreased by two-thirds or so. The rate of development of our agriculture has decreased by about nine tenths....
>
> The seven-year plan has failed. Not only that but with the end of the first ten-year part of our twenty-year plan, none of the quotas have been attained. A tremendous mistake has been made in working out and drawing up the plans. . . .
>
> We have the worst and the most backward productive structure among all the industrially developed countries. . . .
>
> We employ more workers to do repair work than to produce new machines. . . .
>
> In recent years we have seen an enormous accumulation of unsold goods...more than in a year of crisis or depression in the West. . . . The increase in prices in the USSR is taking on inflationary features. . . .
>
> There has not, in fact, been any rise in the standard of

living during recent years. Ten million people have suffered a decrease. . . .

Everything that has been said is highly alarming because it is not just a question of the situation existing in our economy today, but one of the existing trends and this is very, very much worse!

What are its causes? . . .

The principal causes are domestic. First of all, there is the mistaken direction of economic development in which our country is headed. Second of all the systems of planning, incentives, and management of the Soviet economy does not correspond to the real requirements placed upon us. We have been holding doggedly to the line of ultra-industrialization for many years. Even in recent years when there was no longer any necessity to do so, this line of action was continued. . . .

Agriculture. Every year the collective farms have an income which is equivalent in monetary terms to 22 billion rubles. Of this sum, the state takes 11 billion. . . . The average collective farmer can earn 1.50 rubles per day on the collective farms and 3.50 rubles on his own private piece of land. . . .

...we produce more coke than the US but we use three times as much to produce a ton of steel. . . .

Building and housing plans are never fulfilled in the USSR. Housing authorities, as a rule, do not utilize the credits made available to them.

Our systems of planning, establishing incentives and managing industry were developed in the 1930s. Ever since then nothing has changed except the names given things, but in fact, everything remained based on the administrative methods of planning and management. The extreme centralization and the absence of economic democracy have a very serious effect on our economy.

We have an absolute lack of information. The figures published by the Central Statistical Office (ZSU) are blown up....

The ZSU . . . doesn't even have an electronic computer, nor does it have any intention of purchasing one!

Due to the absurd secrecy of much statistical data, the economists are obliged to work in an extremely difficult situation. For example, it is easier for us to obtain any statistical data from American magazines than from the ZSU...Many of the ZSU statistics become absurd if one attempts to analyze them. For example, the ZSU states that we have had a grain harvest of 8 billion pud [1 pud = 36 lbs.]. This is a lie! We have never had any harvest this size.[23]

In a word, the Soviet economic system has reached an advanced

---

23 Agenbegian, A. 1965. *The ASTE Bulletin*, Summer.

stage of obsolescence. The way it handles problems may be illustrated by the parable of the sack of potatoes once related by Michael Polanyi, the distinguished British scholar.

Suppose we have a sack of potatoes and want to make it as compact as possible. One way to do so is to measure the shape of every potato and try to fit all the potatoes together so that they take up the least possible room. This might be done by trial and error or by feeding various measurements into a computer programmed to work out an answer. As any competent mathematician can testify, however, this problem is so complex that it cannot be solved within a reasonable period of time by the most powerful computers. Certainly, no general rules for arranging potatoes can be derived to apply to all possible sacks of them.

Another way to solve the problem is to lift the sack and give it a couple of shakes.

The market as we know it is a marvelous automatic mechanism for shaking countless sacks of potatoes. The millions of participants in the economy adjust to each other by themselves, without being told what to do or where and how to do it.

The Soviet rulers, on the other hand, attempt to organize almost everything in the economy through orders from the top. Under such a system, the number of relations to be managed increases roughly with the square of the different economic activities being undertaken. Some Soviet economists have pointed out that, in order to run the economy in the current fashion two decades from now, the entire adult population would have to be employed just in managing the economy. Nobody would be left over to do the work.

Under the circumstances, it is hardly surprising that agitation for economic reform cracked the surface around five years ago. As in all such matters, the outburst of discussion was not spontaneous but was instead part of a carefully planned official campaign. For a while, however, the long pent-up criticisms that were unleashed threatened to get out of hand. By the time the debate was brought back under control, the existing system had been more severely condemned by Soviet commentators than by many Western observers. This vigorous internal criticism played its part, along with the crop failure of 1963, in altering outside views about the Soviet economy.

The reform movement has come to be associated with the name of Professor E. G. Liberman, but he merely happens to be the man officially chosen to inaugurate the discussion. His proposals are far less radical than those of others, and it would be entirely wrong to label them as "capitalistic." In essence, he is searching for ways to preserve central planning by transferring various routine administrative tasks down to the level of enterprises.

True reforms will come only to the extent that administrative direction of the economy is replaced by markets or quasi-markets. So far, Soviet leaders have not allowed this basic issue to be faced directly in public discussion, because they fear the consequences.

The fact is that reforms are blocked by the age-old "dilemma of the Czars." Like their predecessors, today's rulers recognize that Soviet society is sick, but they know equally well that to cure the patient is to kill the doctor. The economy can be made more efficient only by creating many decision-making centers, dispersing them throughout the economy, and letting them compete impersonally in the marketplace.

But how can the dispersal of economic power be kept from spilling over into the disintegration of the autocratic political order, as it did in Imperial Russia? This is the specter that haunts the Soviet ruling class and paralyzes constructive action. We therefore witness much more talk than action, and the so-called reforms put into effect up to now have not begun to get at the root of the problem.

The economy that surrounds Ivan Ivanov is in many respects simply backward. The facade of industrialization hides many empty and unfinished rooms.

The Soviet Union is just now planning to enter the automobile age, importing the productive know-how from abroad. As the leaders contemplate mass production of automobiles, they must face the reality of a road network smaller than ours before World War I, serving a country two and a half times as large. In the absence of dramatic reforms, the emergence of a modern, progressive, prosperous economy lies a long way down the road.

XI

War and Peace

Ivan must wonder in idle moments, is all this necessary? Why must he work so hard for so little? Why must he live in constant fear of the state, not even enjoying the meager liberties promised to him by the Soviet constitution? Why, in a word, is he condemned to live in his strange world?

Because his rulers tell him, he must serve a cause higher than his own welfare: the cause of history. History dictates, he is told, that Communism is to triumph in an inevitable struggle with capitalism. It is his duty to dedicate himself before all else to hastening the day of that triumph. He is warned to have no illusions: The triumph will come only through protracted warfare and all that it implies.

Half a century ago, Lenin proclaimed that "the existence of the Soviet Republic side by side with imperialist states for a long time is unthinkable. One or the other must triumph in the end. And before that end comes, a series of frightful collisions between the Soviet Republic and bourgeois states will be inevitable."[24] By "imperialist" or "bourgeois" states he meant, of course, nothing more than countries that would resist Soviet domination.

This motif has been repeated countless times in succeeding years, now with this minor variation and now with that, as required by changing circumstance. It has served as the constant guide for foreign policy, even in times of grave emergency when temporary alliances with the "enemy" have proven necessary.

In the curious language of Communism, the most recent form of this policy has taken on the name of "peaceful coexistence," which has nothing to do with either peace or coexistence. It is instead an accommodation of military strategy to the cold facts of power in the modern world.

In the age of nuclear warfare, Soviet leaders view an open clash with the principal non-Communist powers as too dangerous. But, with the collapse of the colonial system, an alternative and safer course seems to have presented itself: instigation of "wars of liberation" around the perimeter. Let the lesser powers fall to

---

24 Lenin. (1919) 1943. "Report of Central Committee at 8th Party Congress." In *Selected Works*. VIII, 33. New York.

Communist control one by one, and perhaps the major powers will realize the inevitability of Communist triumph throughout the world and give in without a struggle. In Communist eyes, "peaceful coexistence" will come about through "peaceful acquiescence."

Khrushchev stated the message clearly. In 1958 he said: "We have always declared and declare now that we do not want war, but we do not renounce class war." The next day he went on to say: "Capitalism is at its ebb, heading for collapse. This does not mean that it is already lying down with its legs stretched out. Much work has yet to be done to bring about such a state."[25]

On another occasion, he stated: "We must realize that we cannot coexist eternally. One of us must go to the grave. We do not want to go to the grave. They do not want to go to their grave either. So what can be done? We must push them to their grave."[26] This is, of course, what he meant by saying, "We shall bury you."

The same point is made less clear though at greater length in a 1960 policy declaration by 81 Communist parties:

> The policy of peaceful coexistence is a policy of mobilizing the masses and launching vigorous action against the enemies of peace. The peaceful coexistence of states does not imply

---

25 Kruschev cited in *Pravda*. 1958. April 9, 1-2.

26 Kruschev cited in Lyons. *Worker's Paradise Lost*, 278.

renunciation of the class struggle. . . . The coexistence of states with different social systems is a form of class struggle between socialism and capitalism. In conditions of peaceful coexistence favorable opportunities are provided for the development of the class struggle in the capitalist countries and the national-liberation movement of the peoples of the colonial and dependent countries. In their turn, the successes of the revolutionary class and national liberation struggle promote peaceful coexistence. The Communists consider it their duty to fortify the faith of the people in the possibility of furthering peaceful coexistence, their determination to prevent a world war. They will do their utmost for the people to weaken imperialism and limit its sphere of action by an active struggle for peace, democracy, and national liberation.[27]

A philosophy so alien to our own is difficult to grasp, and many observers steeped in the democratic tradition have made the dangerous mistake of writing it off as sheer oratory, as sound without meaning. Is it conceivable that a nation's leaders should want to erect a worldwide society on a foundation of hatred? That a conspiratorial mentality could reign over an enormous land for half a century? Is it possible that perpetual warfare with a shadowy

27 1960 policy statement of 81 Communist parties in *Pravda*. 1960. Dec. 6, 4.

"enemy" can be held up as an ideal worth dying for?

Unfortunately, it is. Soviet rulers from Lenin onward have been deadly serious in declaring war on all those who do not passively submit to the Communist "wave of the future." World domination is their goal, and they gain comfort by assuring themselves that they are merely accelerating the destiny of history.

In the Soviet Union, tyranny and conquest are justified in the name of the "scientific laws" of Communism, just as they were in old Russia in the name of the divine right of the Czars. Communism has become throughout the world the modern rationalization for arbitrary power, and this is precisely why would-be dictators everywhere have been so easily brought into the Communist camp. The major Communist powers constitute themselves the grand protectors of lesser dictatorial regimes in exchange for feudal allegiance, much in the ancient way.

In the course of pursuing their grand design, Lenin and his successors have inverted the relationship between diplomacy and warfare. In our tradition, war is viewed as the ultimate and deplorable extension of foreign policy, justifiable only if national security is in peril and all other means of resolving conflicting interests have been exhausted. In the official Soviet mentality, on the other hand, warfare is the normal state of affairs, while foreign policy and diplomacy are among the less costly means of waging it. The object is to force recalcitrants into the Communist fold, to subject them to salvation, not to protect legitimate national interests.

The Soviet campaign against the world has been crowned with many great successes, but recent trends cast doubt on an imminent and final victory. The Soviet empire constructed in the postwar decades is beginning to crack apart. On the one side, the Chinese are pressing for a more vigorous attack against the "enemy." On the other, the people of Eastern Europe are demanding more independence and less belligerence. It remains to be seen whether the policy of invasion and occupation, carried out so tragically in Czechoslovakia, can do more than delay the final reckoning.

Countries like Poland, Hungary, and Czechoslovakia have traditionally been oriented toward the West, economically as well as culturally. Their forced integration into the Soviet bloc of nations, together with the severe restraints placed on their relations with the West, has created an artificial society that few of their leaders consider viable over the long run. Economic and political problems have mounted in recent years, and the pressure for reform of the entire system is building up beyond suppression by the old order.

When asked by a Party official how things were going, a Polish worker supposedly shrugged his shoulders and replied: "Oh, about middling, I'd say, comrade." "Middling? What do you mean by that?" the official asked. The worker answered: "Well, things are worse than last year but better than next."

And then, there are rumblings from within the Soviet Union

itself. While his sovereigns play out their gruesome game of chess with the world as their prize, Ivan Ivanov serves as a tragic pawn. Nobody is more fed up with war than he. Nobody yearns more earnestly for simple tranquillity. He has had quite enough of fighting and killing, whatever the purpose. Over the half-century of Soviet rule, warfare has snuffed out tens of millions of Russian lives and imposed suffering beyond that endured anywhere else.

Is there any chance that Soviet leaders will soon abandon their warped view of the world and become responsible statesmen in pursuit of peace? Or will the frustrations of external relations cause them to turn their attention inward, declaring war on their own and subject nations in a desperate effort to retain absolute power?

In his fearsome vision of 1984, George Orwell saw warfare degenerating into a way of life. He spoke of a time when "war is waged by each ruling group against its own subjects, and the object of the war is not to make or prevent conquests of territory but to keep the structure of society intact. The very word 'war,' therefore, has become misleading. It would probably be accurate to say that by becoming continuous war has ceased to exist. A peace that was truly permanent would be the same as a permanent war. This—although the vast majority of Party members understand it only in a shallower sense—is the inner meaning of the Party slogan: War is Peace."[28]

---

28 Owell, George. 1961. *1984*. New American Library (Signet). New York, 164.

This, also, is the reason for the strange world of Ivan Ivanov.

BIBLIOGRAPHY

The ASTE Bulletin. Indiana University (for the Association for the Study of Soviet-Type Economies). Especially the issue of Summer 1965.

Baron, Salo W. 1964. *The Russian Jew Under Tsars and Soviets*. New York: Macmillan.

Bulletin. Munich: Instiute for the Study of the USSR. Especially issues of June 1967 and November 1967.

DeWitt, Nicholas. 1961. *Education and Professional Employment in the USSR*. Washington: National Science Foundation.

DeWitt, Nicholas. 1955. *Soviet Professional Manpower: Its Education, Training, and Supply.* Washington: National Science Foundation.

Fainsod Merle. 1963. *How Russia Is Ruled*. Cambridge, Mass.: Harvard University Press.

Florinsky, Michael T. 1964. *Russia, a Short History*. New York: Macmillan.

Goodman, Ann S., and Murray Feshbach. 1967. *Estimates and Projections of Educational Attainment in the USSR, 1950-1985.* U.S. Department of Commerce, Bureau of the Census, International Population Reports, Series P-91, No. 16. Washington: Government Printing Office.

Hayward, Max, editor. 1967. *On Trial: The Soviet State versus Abram Tertz" and "Nikolai Arzhak,"* rev. ed. New York: Harper & Row.

Hazard, John N. 1964. *The Soviet System of Government*, 3rd ed. Chicago: University of Chicago Press.

Hazard, John N., and Isaac Shapiro. 1962. *The Soviet Legal System: Post-Stalin Documentation and Historical Commentary*. Dobbs Ferry, N.Y.: Oceana Publications (for Parker School of Foreign and Comparative Law, Columbia University).

Krotkov, Yury. 1967. *The Angry Exile*. London: William Heinemann Ltd.

Kulskii, W. W. 1963. *The Soviet Regime: Communism in Practice*, 4th ed. Syracuse: Syracuse University Press.

Lyons, Eugene. 1967. *Workers' Paradise Lost: Fifty Years of Soviet Communism—A Balance Sheet*. New York: Funk & Wagnalls.

MacAndrew, Andrew R. 1958. "Are Soviet Schools Better Than Ours?" *The Reporter*, Feb. 20.

Novak, Joseph. 1960. *The Future is Ours, Comrade*. Garden City, N.Y.: Doubleday.

Nutter, G. Warren. 1962. *Growth of Industrial Production in the Soviet Union*. Princeton: Priniceton University Press (for National Bureau of Economic Research).

Problems of Communism. Washington: U.S. Information Agency. Especially issues of May–June 1963, Jan.–Feb. 1964, July–Aug. 1964, and March–April 1965.

Salisbury, Harrison, editor. 1967. *The Soviet Union: The Fifty Years*. New York: Harcourt, Brace & World.

Sosnovy, Timothy. 1954. *The Housing Problem in the Soviet Union*. New York: Research Program on the U.S.S.R.

Soviet Studies, A Quarterly Journal on the USSR and Eastern Europe. Glasgow: University of Glasgow. Especially issue of July 1966.

Studies on the Soviet Union. 1967. Munich: Institute for the Study of the USSR. Especially Vol. VI, No. 3.

U.S. Congress. 1959 and 1960. *Comparisons of the United States and Soviet Economics*. Joint Economic Committee. Washington: Government Printing Office.

U.S. Congress. 1962. *Dimensions of Soviet Economic Power*. Joint Economic Committee. Washington: Government Printing Office.

U.S. Congress. 1966. New Directions in the Soviet Economy. Joint Economic Committee. Washington: Government Printing Office.

U.S. Congress. 1955. Trends in Soviet Economic Growth. Joint Economic Committee. Washington: Government Printing Office.

About the Author

G. Warren Nutter (1923-1979) was an American economist who spent the majority of his career at the University of Virginia. Along with James M. Buchanan, he co-founded the Thomas Jefferson Center for Political Economy. Trained at the University of Chicago under Milton Friedman, he specialized in empirical analysis of the Soviet economy. Nutter served as an economic adviser to the Barry Goldwater campaign, and as Assistant Secretary of Defense for International Security Affairs from 1969 to 1973.

About AIER

The American Institute for Economic Research in Great Barrington, Massachusetts, was founded in 1933 as the first independent voice for sound economics in the United States. Today it publishes ongoing research, hosts educational programs, publishes books, sponsors interns and scholars, and is home to the world-renowned Bastiat Society and the highly respected Sound Money Project. The American Institute for Economic Research is a 501c3 public charity.

INDEX

government control, 47-48

persecution of, 49-50, 131-133

Riots in USSR, 43-45

Rule of law, 80, 83

S

Samuelson, Paul, IX

Secret police, Soviet, 44, 75, 78

Sholokhov, Mikhail, 33

Sinyavsky, Andrei, 19, 33-5, 43, 52,
75, 130

Solzhenitsyn, Alexander, 72

Sosnovy, Timothy, 140

Stalin, J. V., XV, 6, 32-33, 50-52, 54,
61, 66, 71, 73, 75, 78-79, 92,
128-30

Standard of living in US and USSR,
139-153

T

Terror, Soviet, 54, 72, 86

Thought control, Soviet, 27, 31, 52, 90

protests against, 33-35, 48

Totalitarianism, 54

Tullock, Gordon, XVII

U

University of Chicago, XI-XIII, XVII

University of Virginia, XIII, XVII, 18

Unrest in USSR, 33-35, 43-45, 69-70,
175-177

V

Venezuela, XVIII

Vishinsky, Andrei, 78

Voluntary Association, US, 38-40,
61-62, 108-109

W

Workbook, Soviet, 114-15

Y

Young Communist League, 42-43, 133

Made in the USA
Middletown, DE
14 September 2021